How to Buy Technology Stocks

Also by Michael Gianturco

Stock Market Investor's Computer Guide

How to Buy Technology Stocks

Michael Gianturco

LITTLE, BROWN AND COMPANY

BOSTON   NEW YORK   LONDON

First Paperback Edition

Previously published as *The Market That Beats the Market*

Some of the material in this book has appeared, in different
form, in *Forbes* magazine. The author is grateful for permission
to include the following previously copyrighted material:
Tables from the Telescan System used by permission of
Telescan, Inc.

Library of Congress Cataloging-in-Publication Data

Gianturco, Michael.
    How to buy technology stocks / Michael Gianturco.
      p.   cm.
    Includes index.
    ISBN 0-316-30997-4
    1. Stocks. 2. High technology industries.   3. Speculation.
    I. Title.
    HG4661.G528   1996
    332.63'22—dc20   96-29117

10 9 8 7 6 5

MV-NY

Printed in the United States of America

This book is for Sydney.

Contents

Preface

EVERY STOCK PURCHASE is an experiment, and I have tried to lay out in this book what has worked during sixteen years of picking and pruning portfolios of science-and-technology stocks. I have kept the discussion basic because the subject is basic. Investing in technology sounds as though it ought to be hard, but there is nothing hard about selecting portfolios of these stocks. When they go up, of course, it becomes a lot of fun.

The most dramatic and in many ways the most instructive technology stock story is that of Compaq Computer. In 1984 it was already widely understood that Compaq was the fastest-growing company the world had ever seen — and yet, adjusting for splits, the stock market valued it at the preposterously low price of $0.58 per share. Ten years later the stock was nudging $42.

Consider what this means. If you had invested $14,000 in Compaq at its 1984 low, you would have become a millionaire in this stock in one decade. Put another way, you would have averaged a *gain* of $100,000 per year for ten years in a row.

The opportunity was easy to miss because it was not at all clear, in 1984, that the American economy was changing in a fundamental way. We can see only in retrospect that Compaq was part of a trickle that would turn into a torrent that would create a great new economic mainstream.

These days, what we still call "the market"—that is, the averaged performance of the thirty mature industrial stocks that go to make up the Dow Jones Industrial Average—is no longer a true reflection of the real economy.

And what we used to regard as a specialized, arcane, somewhat obscure sector of American commerce—the technology group—has essentially *become* the economy. In strong markets in the 1980s and 1990s, the technology stock market has typically doubled the performance of the Dow. It is indeed the market that beats the market. If you invest in this new market, rather than the old one, you can expect to do much better.

How much better? The Dow has returned an averaged 10 percent per year since 1926. For a technology portfolio, I think a realistic target is an averaged annual return of 19 percent, ranging upward for especially lucky or astute investors to 25 percent.

This is not because technology stocks are somehow special. To the contrary: it is because technology is now the norm in an economy that has renewed itself in ways that are not yet fully understood or widely recognized.

The purpose of this book is to identify some rules of thumb for investing wisely in this new economy as it evolves into the next century. I hope you find it helpful.

New York
January 1995

Acknowledgments

I WISH TO THANK James Michaels, Editor of *Forbes* magazine, for valuing the idea of a monthly column on investments in science and technology, and for clear ideas that helped to shape the column as it developed. I would also like to thank my editors at *Forbes*, William Baldwin, Peter Brimelow, William Flanagan, Betty Franklin, and Gary Samuels, for their insights and support over the years.

For their help with this book, many thanks to Michael Pietsch, my editor at Little, Brown and Company, for his thoughtfulness and analytical gifts; to my agent, Russell Galen, for his logic and enthusiasm; and to my family for their patience and interest.

How to Buy Technology Stocks

Introduction:
The New Mainstream

WHEN MICROSOFT'S CHAIRMAN, Bill Gates, became the wealthiest man on the *Forbes* 400 list for the first time, in 1992, there should have been an audible bang. Gates's accession to the top spot on our list made a clear and absolute statement about technology in America, to wit: what we used to think of as the technology sector of the economy — a sort of curious, arcane, and specialized business off to one side, a nerd business — had *become* the economy.

And for the first time an intellectual young person — not an athlete, not an entertainer — had somehow parlayed a work of the mind (some lines of code, a pure abstraction) into the greatest private fortune in the country: $7 billion. This was a personal net worth greater than that accumulated by any other person in America, by any other means. Unlike the earlier great fortunes of the twentieth and nineteenth centuries, the Microsoft money did not arise from the manufacture or transport of hard things, nor was it pumped out of the ground. No. This new money came gushing straight out of a brain. Bill Gates's fortune is not unique in this regard. Great personal fortunes are now being fitted together by business visionaries who know how to tap into the intellectual resources of biotechnology, networking, and a few other rather deeply abstract pursuits.

For stock and fund investors, there is a practical everyday lesson to be taken from Bill Gates and his kindred capitalists. It must be understood from their entrepreneurial successes that the rules of the investing game have changed markedly, and that a new type of portfolio is very much in order.

The formerly industrial economy of the United States, an economy in which most real wealth has for centuries originated in the resources of the earth, has been transformed. New wealth now appears to arise directly from the resources of the mind. Mining and manufacturing have been displaced, in the scale of profitable pursuits, by coding and decoding. Coding computers — decoding genes. As financial assets and information are increasingly transferred and banked electronically, the coding and decoding of money itself has become a paramount concern.

Investors who hearkened to these trends have done very well indeed. For example, Microsoft's stock began trading in March 1986 at a split-adjusted $2.33. A recent top was $95. If you had bet $1,000 on the initial offering, it would have been worth $39,772 only seven years later.

Stock in Amgen, a tiny but ferociously competitive biotechnology company in Thousand Oaks, California, traded near $9 as it wrestled a major pharmaceutical house in court for the rights to a new antianemia drug. When Amgen won, the stock rose like a balloon cut free to $90 — a tenfold gain in less than two years. Compaq Computer, launched by twenty-five venturesome engineers in rented space on the third floor of a bank in suburban Northwest Houston, became within two years the fastest-growing company in the history of the world. If you missed these winning stocks, this book is intended to help you find the next ones.

Such examples of energetic and enthusiastic capitalism are all the more striking because they have been acted out against a backdrop of industrial decline and shrinking employment. In the past twenty years, Americans have witnessed at firsthand episodes of collapse or crisis in many major industries: aircraft and automobile manufacturing, consumer electronics, steel production, mining, and even — perhaps most ominously — in banking. We have also seen major crashes and recoveries in the stock market, and the bursting of enormous speculative bubbles in oil, precious metals, real estate, "emerging market" funds, junk bonds, and derivatives. Pop pop pop.

Yet there is nothing wrong with the economy. It exists, like any organism that has life, in a dynamic state of decline and renewal. Over time the economy slowly changes, so that suddenly one day it is possible to scan back over a decade or two and realize, in a flash of insight, that things are different now.

Many social and economic observers have taken such a sighting. They have generally concluded that we now live in a "postindustrial society." This tells us what the society is not. What it has actually become, over a period of decades, is a deeply technological society. Technology is in fact the new mainstream of this new economy. Science is its jetstream.

It surprises and intrigues many investors to learn that picking science-and-technology stocks and funds is actually rather straightforward — even easy. When the pick is correct and they go up, of course it becomes fun. You can be utterly indifferent to or bored by technology and still make quite a lot of money in these stocks.

As an undergraduate I majored in English literature. I learned something that is helpful in investing in technology stocks, and here it is. In a novel, the apparent story — the superficial tale that keeps you turning the pages — is formulaic, predictable and largely trivial. The real story is always hidden beneath the surface. The lesson is useful in stock picking. When you look at a tech stock, it is the story behind the story that counts. The superficial story — the one you will be told — is understood to be trivial.

For example, as a technology investor you will be asked to believe, again and again and in wholly different contexts, the Great Napkin Myth. This stock story goes that the founders of the XYZ company got together one evening in a (bar, cafe, Chinese or Mexican restaurant, pick one) and doodled out on a napkin their astonishing new design for a (semiconductor, desktop computer, catalytic reaction system, pick one). Miraculously, the product simply took off. Now confronted with the problems of unbridled revenue growth, the founding doodlers are seeking public funding (from *you*, actually) in order to build great storage bins to capture and retain their incoming cash flow, to construct new factories, to recruit marketing personnel, et cetera.

"Designed on a napkin" is a concept that should be received with a smile and in exactly the same spirit as the phrase "brought by the stork." It is not precisely true. More likely, the two founders slipped out the side door of their employer's (semiconductor, computer, chemical) plant with a pirated design for a new product, and were met in the parking lot by a very interested venture capitalist. This is how small technology companies are typically born — from the side door of a large technology company. The napkin myth neatly covers this, along with some other difficulties, such as: the founders went into business on the pilfered design, made quite a lot of money thanks to the zeroed research and development costs attendant on product theft — but have now run all the way through that product's life cycle and have no clear idea how to develop a new one.

They are being sued by their former employer and they are out of money, in trouble at the bank, and must now either go public or go bankrupt. In other words, science-and-technology investing is not all sweetness and light, industrial progress and Horatio Alger. I am not urging cynicism. There are not too many such stinkers among technology stock offerings, and one should remain sympathetic to the technology enterprise. It is indeed a basis for human progress as well as investment profits. But when you read a prospectus or annual report, make it a habit to ignore the surface story and read deeply between the lines.

In my experience, common sense and perhaps even a little measured distaste for science and technology might help in picking winners among these stocks. If you loathed physics in high school, for instance, you will probably do better at this than the kid who was president of the science club. This is because an uncritical enthusiasm for science and technology will almost certainly trip you up as an investor. A friendly but businesslike skepticism seems the most productive outlook. The right answers to a few simple, nontechnical litmus-test questions will keep your portfolio out of trouble and help assure good results.

If you can play the familiar board game Monopoly, you are already well grounded, for science-and-technology stocks rise and fall on their ability to capture and protect their markets from competition. It is their special ability to create and protect new monopolies, and to shatter old ones, that makes technology companies so exceptionally profitable as investments. (For example, IBM created a colossal monopoly; Apple shattered it.) The difficult, leaden, often profoundly dull technical details of a specific commercial technology, whatever it happens to be, are largely trivial to the investor. It is the *monopolies* that produce profits — not the chips, the codes, the nucleic acids, or the lasers.

When you are faced with buying the stock of a technology company bearing one of those absurdly pretentious, newly coined Martian names (like, say, Xylogicor or Trigenisynth), do not be intimidated or dissuaded. What you are really buying into is good old Marvin Gardens, Park Place, or Atlantic Avenue.

You don't have to look very hard to find science and technology stocks for sale. There are thousands, and hundreds of new issues are being created as the economy continues to transform and renew itself. The investor's problem is simply one of elimination. The rules for not buying technology stocks will guide you past a thousand turkeys to the very few stocks you should actually consider holding.

These new rules are quite different from the traditional rules used by stock investors for valuing conventional and mature industrial companies. The most basic rules for figuring out how much to pay for a stock have changed. The new rules are actually simpler; but they must be understood. This book describes the new rules and explains the mistakes (and scams) to avoid, steps to take, procedures to follow, and very simple formulas to apply. It also suggests when to sell.

What to expect? In a portfolio of science-and-technology stocks, a realistic expectation for averaged annual gain is 19 percent to 25 percent. Skillful and lucky technology investors not uncommonly enjoy a +100 percent year every now and then, and even this is not the upper limit.

If you trade options on the more volatile technology stocks, you are probably well aware that with a $100 initial stake, you are never more than six trades away from $1.5 million. (You have to be right six times in a row, and the odds against it are truly steep. But you already know that, too.)

No one would want to rule out the possibility of such an enormous, life-altering short-term gain — but more to the point for most investors is the need to rule out the prospect of diminishing returns on their existing, late-twentieth century industrial stock portfolios: what can you expect of a portfolio that is not trimmed, right now, to track the sea changes affecting the economy? Precious little. A performance disappointingly trailing off into the next century.

At the end of the last century, most of the stocks traded on the New York Stock Exchange were railroad shares. In the afterglow of the industrial revolution, it was difficult for investors to even conceive of the looming changes that were already evident. Internal combustion, motorcars, primitive flight, and the distribution and application of electricity were not merely forthcoming at the end of the nineteenth century — they were altogether obvious. But in the 1890s, an investor asked to foresee the technological future would almost certainly have predicted further marvels from the miracle of steam propulsion, and continued to lard his portfolio with the common stocks of nineteenth-century railway networks. We all tend to predict the present.

The marvel of the present age — our own vaunted steam engine, the semiconductor — will be fifty years old in this decade. This technology and the terms that so enthusiastically described its era — such as *high technology* — will not be forever young. This is not to say the semiconductor will be supplanted the day after tomorrow by some more advanced switching technology, although this is possible. Rather, the point is that investments in technology need a fresh look. The descriptive salute "hi-tech" is already in decline and will one day go the way of "hi-fi." In other words, if you hear it from a broker, be a little wary.

Similarly, the investment slogans and formulas for describing growth and technology stocks developed over the past half-century — stock market clichés based largely on the 1960s and 1970s miracles of the transistor and the microchip — no longer apply, and they certainly won't bridge the turn of the century. As stock buyers, we need new ideas and new yardsticks. The questions you must ask as an investor never vary. What to buy? At what price? And when to sell it? The answers have certainly changed, and the methods for discovering these answers are markedly different today from those of a decade ago.

We are in a period of enormous and unsubtle change. Spotting and understanding the trends is not particularly difficult. Identifying specific stocks as vehicles to help profit by these trends is harder — but not nearly as daunting as one might suppose. Simple rules presented in this book will help you eliminate stocks unworthy of investment. When you have narrowed it down to a few good stocks or funds, the choices are clear and easy to make.

This is because *technology* and *technology stocks* are two entirely different subjects. You don't have to know what DNA stands for in order to successfully buy it low and sell it high. You do have to know how to spot a good value — and this investing principle is timeless, nontechnical, and immune to obsolescence. The object of the game is the same, but the rules are changing.

This book is intended to help you find good stock values, and names specific stocks, funds, and groups to help you get started. The emphasis is on science-and-technology stocks because no other in-vestment group will benefit so directly— and so handsomely — as the future unfolds. Technology and science are, respectively, our present and our future. And so too are common stocks in companies based upon new science and fresh technologies.

PART ONE

THE
TECHNOLOGY
STOCK MARKET

Chapter 1

Getting Started

A S A FIRST STEP, subtract your age from 100. For example, if you are 40, the result will be 60. This number represents the percentage of your assets you should hold in stocks or in funds of stocks.

If you want to invest in the market that beats the market, you should proceed gradually. If you are a complete neophyte, a sensible first move would be to position your entire stock portfolio in a market that *cannot do worse* than the market — that is, in the Standard & Poor's 500. A number of mutual fund companies offer funds that are indexed to the S&P 500. They are called, loosely, the "index funds." The Vanguard Group offers such a fund and is a strong advocate of the concept. Management fees are quite reasonable because the funds are not actively managed.

If you buy shares in an index fund, it is as though you had purchased shares in each of the 500 stocks that go to make up the index. When "the market" goes up, as indicated by a rise in the S&P 500 index, the value of your shares will go up in lockstep with it. When it goes down, your shares will do likewise. The gain in this broad market since the twenties has averaged about 10 percent per year. This is a good platform, a good place to park. As you purchase technology stocks and funds over time, you can tap this reservoir of money that you know will perform precisely as well as the broad market. No better but no worse.

In this example of a forty-year-old, of the 60 percent of investable assets earmarked for stocks and funds, about one-fifth of the equity "pie" should be transferred rapidly into technology stocks or high-growth technology funds. This means that at the end of a year or at most two years, depending on the vigor of the markets, you should try to achieve an 80/20 split between your index fund position and your high-growth science-and-technology stock position. Note that it is when the market is weak — so weak that people don't even want to talk about it — that you should be buying technology. If the air is filled with excitement and the market is exploding, then ride the index fund up and bide your time. Bad times will surely come again, and it is in the purple-black funks of the down markets that you should be making purchases.

Beyond the 80/20 split between your index fund and your technology stock allocation, you must exercise additional judgment and care, because you are taking on more risk by *leading* the S&P 500. By this I mean you will be shifting into technology stocks faster than the index does. At root, this means you will be moving money into technology faster than the economy does. Yet we will not be very deep into the twenty-first century when some seer announces that the S&P 500 has evolved into a science-and-technology stock index. It is strongly trending that way right now. If you shift funds out of an index fund and into technology funds, you are anticipating the direction the market and the economy must go. Technology is the future. This has been a reliable truism since the Stone Age.

Should you use mutual funds or stocks? Both. Use an index fund, as noted, as an initial position or platform, and then move into selected technology stocks or funds. Buy the funds directly from the fund company, not through a bank or broker. Buy stocks through a "name" discount brokerage such as Quick & Reilly, Fidelity, or Schwab, or even through a full-service broker. If you find that you are so concerned about the cost of commissions that you must seek out a bargain-basement brokerage, then consider the possibility that you are trading too much.

Here are three important traps to avoid. (1) Never pay a "load," or commission, on a fund purchase. Insist on "no-load" funds. (2) Never pay for something called a "wrap fee," that is, a fixed annual management fee in lieu of trade-by-trade commissions. (3) Never accept a "lock-up" — a fee structure that penalizes you for withdrawing capital from the fund. You need not have an attorney at your elbow to spot these problems. Just pipe up boldly and ask pointed questions like, "Can I get my money out of this thing without paying you guys a penalty?" If not, keep shopping.

Finally, how can you tell you are really buying technology? The concept of a technology stock has been with us for several decades, and the technology label is still stuck fast to some declining companies whose wares and services have long since sunk into obsolescence.

As a first cut, it helps to think a moment about *moving parts*. Modern technology companies offer products and services based on moving parts that are too tiny to see (photons, electrons, molecules) or are pure abstractions (lines of code, decoded gene sequences, encoding algorithms). If the company you're investing in sells a product with moving parts that are big enough to see with the naked eye, like a gear or a piston, you're probably not investing in an advanced technology.

The most important thing to recognize in this connection is that technology per se is not really what you want to invest in. You want to invest in companies that can produce exceptional profits. By this I mean they should be able to achieve and sustain net margins of 18 percent to 25 percent or better. Technology companies are able to do this because they can so readily create natural or formal monopolies. There is nothing inherently wonderful about newness. New technologies are attractive investments, not because they are "hot" or modish, but because new things are easy to protect with patents or proprietary knowledge. An important patent, for example, can assure a run of legitimate monopoly profits that will be sustainable for seventeen years.

It is the technology-based monopoly and the profits that can follow from it, and not merely the technology, that should attract you as an investor. This book will provide guidelines to help you identify stocks in science and technology that have exceptional profit potential.

Chapter 2

When to Buy

THE BEST TIME TO BUY technology stocks is at three in the afternoon on Monday in the week of Thanksgiving day. This is not a joke.

Technology stocks usually mount a vigorous rally between the end of November and the end of January. In the past three years the average gain for the technology group has been +15 percent in this two-month period, so it is a vigorous updraft. The first sign of the rally is a holiday upturn preceding Thanksgiving.

With this most basic timing tool as a point of departure, this chapter will explain how to use several other easy-to-read cycles in science-and-technology industries and stocks. Some helpful rules emerge. For example: when semiconductor stocks are weak, any technology stock can be bought with confidence. When software stocks are a runaway success, it is time to take profits in every stock group. And when the dollar is weakening, it is a good time to buy biotech.

Investing in the perennial winter rally in the science-and-technology sector seems like an idea that is too simple to work, and yet it does. The first signs of the rally usually appear as a normal holiday upturn preceding the approach of Thanksgiving day. Monday, which is typically a downish day in any market week, is likely to be the last blah day before the rally starts — so a Monday-morning decline should create bargains for you to buy in the late afternoon.

Buy at the market price no later than three o'clock. This way, your broker will have plenty of time to get your orders executed before the close and before institutional buyers — who typically reserve their orders until the last hour of trading — can bid up the stocks on your shopping list to inordinately high entry prices.

The reasons for the year-end rally in small capitalization stocks, including the science-and-technology stocks, have been examined repeatedly and at length in academic studies over many years. In the specific case of hardware technology stocks, such as semiconductors, electronics, and computers, underlying seasonal and inventory cycles in these businesses would seem to contribute to the big winter rally.

But no one really knows why the rally happens. It has been explained in various ways and has also been explained away completely. In other words, whether this so-called January Effect on stock prices actually exists remains an open question. I will continue to trade on it because it continues to make money. One could generalize from this purely practical, stock trader's point of view that this most expectable rally may occur simply because so many market players expect it.

In any event, year after year the winter rally has proved a reliable play. It is a useful place to start if you wish to reconfigure your portfolio as we approach the turn of the century. This is because the annual rally in the science-and-technology sector happily coincides with the tax-loss selling season.

During this year-end period, investors with substantial losses who have elected to take those losses, rather than wait them out, sell in order to realize the loss in the current year. Tax selling puts a psychological drag on the whole market, and may even diminish the prices — and enhance the attractiveness — of stocks you want to buy. If you are exiting some heavy twentieth-century industrials that may have disappointed you in the course of the year, you might wish to redeploy the cash you raise at their sale into a few good science-and-technology stocks.

A few stocks means three or four per year. And here is the second basic timing rule affecting decisions on when to buy. Spread your purchases over time. Don't jump in with both feet. By buying into technology gradually, on an annual basis, you can automatically avoid putting too much money into the merely fashionable technology or hot scientific idea of any particular year. The idea of temporal diversification — that is, diversifying your portfolio across time as well as industry group — is bedrock-solid advice, particularly in a field that changes as rapidly as technology. Curiously, it is advice rarely offered and even more rarely taken. Uninvested cash drives people crazy.

It drives brokers crazy because any cash that is just sitting in your account, in a money market fund or in T-bills, is eminently portable. Brokers know that you could easily and without consequence pull it out of your account if the market should happen to go sour. In contrast, money already invested in stocks is money that has been trapped. Cash drives investors crazy because it just sits there, uninvested and (while a rally lasts) unproductive.

The most tempting course of action for most of us — particularly when stocks are hot and our friends are reporting at parties that *they* are making lots of money on stocks or stock funds — is to plunge into the market all at once with all available resources. Such an optimistic move will delight your broker or fund rep, but it is of course one of those soon-to-be-regretted enthusiasms. Regrets arise as the market snakes downward the very next day.

The bad part of a market decline is not, in the final analysis, the decline in stock prices. Stocks go down and up. Over time, they go up more than they go down. Since 1926, the broad market has oscillated around a trendline that climbs about 10 percent per year. The market for science-and-technology stocks is relatively new, but it commonly does about twice as well as the S&P. If you lose money on a downswing you'll probably get it back, plus a bit, on the next upswing. So holding some money back from the market is not suggested here as a strategy to avoid losing that money — you probably wouldn't.

Rather, the reason to commit funds to the market a little at a time is that you will have some cash in hand to meter into the market on the inevitable downswings. You can in this way pick up additional shares at sunken price levels. If you are a typical investor you will probably sell stocks very rarely, so it is especially important for you to buy them well. Chapter 3 will develop the idea that while marking time between technology stock purchases, one good place to park any cash reserve is in utility stocks or funds.

So, there are only two workable calendar rules I know for timing investments in science and technology: buy just before Thanksgiving, and spread your purchases over time. If calendar-based rules were a dead-reliable guide, traders might try to do more with them. Given the occasion of the January Effect rally, for example, one might reasonably hope to anticipate a January Aftereffect — a sort of hangover period, from February to April, when traders take profits and stocks plateau or sink.

In some years there may actually be such a hangover period, but it is not tradable. If you were to bet on such a downtrend as though it were predicted by a formula, it would probably turn out that your specific stocks would not be affected, and you would end up selling too soon for a superfluous and silly reason. With the single exception of the January Effect rally, it is probably best to consider the business cycle in timing your stock purchases and sales, rather than any sort of stock market cycle. Ignore the great body of trading lore about what is supposed to happen to the markets in the spring, summer, and fall. It is a great body of clichés.

Notice, for example, that the market does not rise every summer in a muscular "summer rally," nor does it always sink into a "summer slump" or crash altogether in a "summer swoon." It does not collapse every October in an annual "October crash." And it does not invariably sell off in the tax-selling season of early winter — for sometimes that selling season coincides with, and is perfectly offset by, the well-known "Santa Claus Rally."

To the extent that it follows any sort of cycle, the stock market moves, not between summer and winter, but between boom and bust. Day one of a stock market cycle is not January 1. It is the day — whatever day — a recession's end is finally sighted.

Here is a firmer basis for deciding when to buy. There exists a basic technology business cycle. It is not as simple and seasonal as, say, grain prices. But it does follow certain reliable patterns. There is a good time to buy semiconductors, a good time to buy software stocks, and a good time to buy nothing at all. The original observation of these patterns has been attributed to an executive at DataQuest in San Jose. He is not a stock market watcher. His life's work has consisted of gathering and analyzing sales, inventory, and distribution statistics on technology-based businesses. In other words, he watches the real world.

His economic insight was this: when technology business improves, the recovery is most noticeable at first in the order books of the semiconductor companies. The strengthening business cycle next blesses the computer companies — and then, finally, benefits software companies. His original expectation was that technology stock

groups should follow suit, rising one after the other like three successive squadrons launched from the deck of an aircraft carrier: semiconductors first, then computers, then software.

Viewed as a clock on the market for technology stocks, the concept
is very helpful. It tells us that the first signal of a major rally is a sharp
runup in semiconductor stocks. If you should happen to miss that one,
you might still (theoretically, anyway) invest in anticipation of subsequent rallies in the computer and software groups. And when you notice the software stocks are very much elevated — toppy and wobbly —
you know it is time to take profits on the whole group.

The theory makes excellent sense, but you cannot directly apply it
as a short-term trading strategy. The reason is that as soon as the semiconductor rally is clearly under way, everything else happens in a
whoosh. In a strong business recovery, the stock market, having seen
step one, doesn't wait around for the other two.

It is also true that in recent years, the semiconductor industry has
begun to subsume the computer business — it is in fact becoming the
computer business. This is fundamentally altering the cycle, and in
the most recent go-round, it appeared that semiconductor stocks enjoyed a double rally: once in their own right, and a second time as a
proxy for the computer sector. As usual, things are not as simple as
one might wish. So many other cycles (and events) are superimposed
on the basic, three-phase technology business cycle that it is exceed-
ingly difficult to guess from business statistics what specific actions, if
any, should be taken in the stock market.

It certainly helps, however, to know the underlying pattern is
there. At the very beginning and the very end of the grand cycle, the
signs can indeed be seen clearly. A sudden explosion in semiconductors tells you the cycle is beginning to turn up. When semiconductors
are bottoming out, computer manufacturers' stocks are in decline,
and software stocks are peaky — watch out. The end is nigh. What
may well follow is a business recession in the technology stock group,
and what will almost certainly follow is a nosedive in software stock
prices.

For the long-term investor, the most useful signals that may arise
from this cyclic view of the technology businesses is the clear-cut buy-
it-all signal generated by a rally in semiconductor stocks. It is sometimes possible to anticipate this crucial, bellwether rally by keeping an
eye on the stocks of small companies that sell capital equipment to the
semiconductor industry. Good examples of such indicator stocks are

KLA Instruments, Silicon Valley Group, and Lam Research. Such companies are the first to benefit from an upturn in this sector of the economy, and their stocks are the crocuses and forsythia of the technology stock market.

It would seem that the business cycle of the electronics-based computer, semiconductor, and software industries would have nothing to do with the unrelated stocks of the biotechnology, medical device, and pharmaceutical groups.

Curiously, however, there is a seesaw relationship among these stocks that can be useful to investors. Twice since the mid-1980s, severe declines in the stocks of computer-related companies have been accompanied by simultaneous strong rallies in the biotech stocks. Portfolios constructed to carry an equal weighting of both types of stocks can certainly benefit from this type of diversification. Computers go way down, biotechs go way up — and then they reverse the dance. A portfolio invested in both groups will grow on an even keel under passive management — that is, without a lot of (costly, nervous, twitchy) buying and selling.

If you are a more adventurous or active manager of your own stocks, or if you trade in and out of the technology-sector mutual funds, you might wish to consider shifting the weighting of your portfolio back and forth between computer-related technologies and biotechnologies. There are two ways to time these shifts.

Generally, if the economy appears to be weakening, the medical-related stocks become more attractive as safe havens, and the computer-based stocks go soft on declining earnings. This is an intriguing and seemingly obvious observation, made in retrospect, but it is a very hard call for any observer to make while these trends are falling into place. One clear signal of a weakening economy is a sharp, sudden runup in the so-called defensive stocks, including the medical, biotech, and pharmaceutical issues. But it is not really much help to investors, since this runup in stocks is also precisely the trend we would hope to anticipate, capture, and profit by.

A more practical, formulaic approach is to watch the value of the dollar relative to other currencies. Biotechnology companies in the United States are largely private research laboratories in the act of becoming pharmaceutical companies. Many of them are heavily dependent upon research spending by established pharmaceutical companies. These companies are among the strongest of U.S. exporters.

A few of the largest biotech companies have now established

themselves as pharmaceutical manufacturers in their own right — so they, too, share the dollar sensitivity of the pharmaceutical business. A weak dollar helps domestic pharmaceutical makers gain ground against overseas competitors. A strong dollar hurts their exports. As the dollar declines, shifting a technology portfolio in the direction of biotech and pharmaceutical stocks makes sense.

The effect of a stronger dollar on U.S.-based computer-related businesses is less clear cut, but it is also somewhat significant. The electronics industry has exported its labor-intensive tasks to factory sites dotted around the Pacific rim and across Latin America. The value of the dollar affects them in the same way it affects foreign companies that import goods into the United States.

These companies exchange foreign-made goods for dollars, and a strong dollar against weak foreign currencies has the happy effect of cutting their manufacturing costs. A strengthening dollar also accompanies a strengthening U.S. economy. So it is a good idea, when the dollar firms, to sell some biotech and pharmaceutical stocks, and roll the proceeds of these sales back into computer-related stocks.

Is it necessary to examine the value of the dollar every day in order to invest in science-and-technology stocks? Hardly. These observations are simply available to you, whenever you feel like checking, to help you form your decision to buy, take a profit, or get rid of a loser. A technology portfolio is like any other investment portfolio in that the best course, most of the time, is to do nothing at all.

What about the economy?

Computer-related technology stocks have an attractively simple quality. They move up and down in synchrony with the economy. When times are good they go up; when times are bad they go down. They actually do what many naive investors expect of the whole stock market.

Yet, if you have observed the Dow Jones Industrial Average or the bond markets through a few business cycles, you will have noticed that they pass through long periods in which good news for human beings is received as terrible news for the markets, and vice versa. Late in a business recession, news of stronger housing starts, upbeat purchasing managers' reports, higher employment, and improving retail sales all have the effect of clobbering the Dow.

This seems irrational on the face of it, but it is not. An improving economy brings increased competition for money, that is, investable capital. The price of capital, which is the interest rate, naturally rises in response to this heightened competition for money. As interest rates go up, the Dow goes down.

Income-oriented investors reason that if they can get good yields from debt instruments, which are risk free, then why leave cash at risk in the stock market in the hope of receiving the same rate of return in the form of dividends? Thus, the Dow stocks lose their appeal as the competition for capital heats up, and the Dow sells off just as springtime comes to the business world.

At the other end of the business cycle, as the economy contracts into recession, businesses no longer need capital for expansion. The price of money therefore declines, and the Dow stocks' dividends begin to look relatively attractive. The Dow invariably rises into recession. Because the market for large-capitalization, dividend-paying stocks is 180 degrees out of phase with the economy, experienced investors go into an automatic doublethink when the economy begins to change direction. For investors in blue-chip stocks, good news equals bad news — and bad news is to be understood as a buy signal.

The refreshing thing about technology stocks is that this ingrained habit of thought — this odd, professional mental trick of reversing the significance of almost everything that happens — does not logically apply. Science-and-technology growth stocks rarely pay dividends at all, and many of them, thanks to successful public offerings or good business performance, are perched atop enormous hoards of cash.

As interest rates go up, technology companies make better returns on their invested cash. And since they pay no dividends, they are rarely held by income-oriented investors and institutions. A stock that is not owned cannot be sold.

In short, unlike the Dow stocks, technology growth stocks are not likely to be dumped in favor of debt instruments when interest rates rise. The price of a technology growth stock goes up in proportion as the company grows. In boom times the business grows faster. In this particular corner of the stock market, good news is *not* bad news. Good news is good news.

If you are a natural optimist, you have a split-second advantage in this field of investing over most seasoned stock traders. Your direct, intuitive instinct to buy a technology stock on good economic news is precisely the right one. Good news is a harbinger of good gains in technology stock prices. To get this straight, most market mavens have to double back on their normal, wired-in habit of reversing good news to bad. Chances are good that in the time it takes them to parse through the problem and figure out which way to play the economic news, you will have already bought the stock.

Periods of economic resurgence are good times to buy technology stocks, but they are not the only times you can profit by buying against the prevailing negative sentiment of market professionals. Suppose you open the financial papers one morning and learn that a high-visibility technology company has just reported appalling quarterly earnings, lost 20 percent of its market value, and will probably *never*, in the view of the writer, come back. When you see one of these never-come-back articles (and they are a set piece of business journalism), you should wait a day or two and then buy the stock.

How do journalists arrive at such a dire and absolute view of such matters? They interview stock analysts in the research departments of brokerages. In a damning article of this kind, an analyst who is urging his clients to sell the stock is usually directly quoted or at least cited by name. This tells you where the idea came from.

Analyst rhymes with *loyalist*. Analysts rarely recommend selling a stock until that stock has been run down for so long, and has sunk so pitifully, that it has become a personal albatross: they want it released from their lists and their reputations. A sell recommendation from a high-profile analyst directly engenders selling among the brokerage's own institutional and other customers. Short sellers leap onto the bandwagon.

Rival brokerages follow suit, if only to shift their own customers to safety. The stock drops dramatically, then drastically. The press naturally notices this, and the never-come-back articles ensue, recycling the sell recommendations of the analysts to national mass audiences. The widespread casting away of the stock ends at this point, because everyone who might wish to sell has already heard the news and sold. The selling pressure is exhausted. That's the bottom. That's when to buy.

These very public buy signals are most likely to occur in the period beginning three weeks after the end of the close of a major financial reporting quarter. Watch for them from January 15, April 15, July 15, and October 15.

Chapter 3

What to Buy

TECHNOLOGY COMPANIES CAN SUCCEED spectacularly, and their prototypes are legendary. Xerox, Hewlett-Packard, IBM, Apple, Intel, Microsoft, Amgen, Compaq — the list goes on. Brokers naturally rely on these past successes as metaphors for the particular stocks they happen to be selling. For example, a new biotech issue will invariably be presented as "another Amgen" just as, a decade ago, it seemed that every growth stock in the brokers' inventory was to be understood at some subtle level as "another Xerox."

There is nothing wrong with learning from past triumphs in the stock market, but when you examine more closely the history of technology stocks, it becomes clear there are two different types of success stories: short ones and long ones.

Short success stories typically characterize small, single-product companies with a bright idea and a lucky sense of timing. Maybe the product is a program, maybe it's a chip. In a first step, the product succeeds splendidly, the company is brought public, and the stock takes flight on dramatic revenue growth and good profits.

In a second step, the drama of success magnetizes the attention of competitors, who surge into the field with comparable products at sharply reduced prices. The business contracts, the stock plummets. The typical cycle is completed in as little as two years.

Current technologies are dead-easy to copy. Electronics manufacturing *is* copying — it is a largely photographic process — and replicating a photographic process is not much more difficult than snapping a picture. Software is manufactured by copying floppy disks. The distinction between production by copying and copying a product is now almost entirely an ethical one.

In the 1940s, a manufacturer of, say, tractors was protected from would-be competitors by the high capital cost of the unique tooling and machinery capable of compelling raw steel to assume the unique and intricate shapes of tractor parts. But modern tooling is likely to be weightless and cheap — a few hundred lines of code written by a programmer will quickly transform a numerically controlled machine tool into a tractor-part manufacturing machine. Tooling cost does not raise much of an obstacle to competition, so a ferocious buzz of competition arises very quickly around any one manufacturer's commercial success. If the novel concept in technology cannot be protected, somehow, its creator is in for a very short season.

The purpose of technological innovation is to make things easier and cheaper. The great trick for any technology-based business is to keep from being carried away by this wonderful progressive trend to easiness and cheapness — so carried away that the company's own innovation and production work becomes devalued, as its stock sinks below the horizon line. As an investor you should try to discover technology companies whose managements and stocks can resist the product downpricing that fresh technology promises and, ultimately, inevitably, devastatingly delivers. It is easy, not hard, to go into a technology manufacturing business. It's staying in business that's tough.

A good recent example of what can happen is the introduction of the fax modem, a device that lets computer users send and receive faxes on their computers. The business limped along for a decade and then suddenly exploded. In one year in the early 1990s, more than fifty companies suddenly jumped into the manufacture of fax modems. With so much new competition, modem prices naturally plummeted. From early prices near $600, modem retail prices dropped to the $200 range, hung there briefly, then sank below $100. As competitors poured into this new field, the price of each successive modem generation declined. Not surprisingly, earnings declined, and when earnings contract, stock prices fall. After just three years of this competitive turmoil, Lisa Thompson, an articulate research analyst at Punk, Ziegel & Knoll in New York, characterized the scene as "the heartbreak of the fax modem hardware market."

The modems traced a typical hardware technology business trajectory. Early great success is often self-liquidating, because it attracts competition and the barriers to entry are low or nonexistent. As a general rule, vigorous competition does not strengthen small technology companies. It kills them.

In any competition, however ferocious, somebody wins. An original, very clever faxing program, called WinFax (the product that probably triggered the fax modem boom), became within two years the prototype for thirteen other packaged and published commercial ripoffs of its basic program design. In this case, however, the original product and its manufacturer, Delrina, survived and ultimately triumphed.

A first marketer of a new idea always has a so-called natural monopoly: the competition has not yet turned up. Strong selling during this short, early grace period can build the platform for a longer-term success. The originator can often retain the lion's share of the market even after the piggyback riders turn up. By 1994, Delrina's share of market was estimated at somewhere between 66 percent and 90 percent. (Technology market research is not, we notice, grounded on exact numbers; but the point is, Delrina essentially owned the business.)

It costs much more to buy share of market than it does to simply keep it, so the inventor of a technology does have an inherent advantage. Delrina was able to draw capital strength from other lines of products and from public offerings of stock. They surfed on the success of Microsoft's Windows, which coincided with their own and supported it. They endured the competitive firestorm, outlasted and ultimately licensed in some of their exhausted competition. Most recently they have reconceived their product as a service — that is, as a "front end" for networked fax services. They sold four million copies of WinFax, and at this writing they are still selling them at the rate of 250,000 per month.

Capital strength, endurance, and linking technology to networks are all important elements of survival and success in technology marketing, as we shall see.

What is the quality common to the long-term stock market success stories? They invariably revolve around stocks in companies that have secured at least a limited monopoly. Microsoft, Cisco Systems, Novell, and Intel have been good examples. All are, or have been at some point in their history, near-monopolies. IBM was a splendid monopoly and had the longest-running success story in recent memory. When the monopoly broke, the story ended. Nothing could have restored it.

Parenthetically, it is impossible to write in a realistic way about technology without invoking the subject of monopoly. A monopoly is defined as the solitary control of a product or service and its market. Implied in this definition is the power to control price or, bluntly put, to keep prices high. Unlimited monopolies are extremely rare birds. It is therefore customary among business writers to qualify the term *monopoly* in some way. We crutch along on "limited monopoly" or "virtual monopoly" or apply more sharply defined words, such as *hegemony* or *duopoly* or *oligopoly.*

This is going to be a long essay, however, so let's simply make an understanding that whenever the word *monopoly* appears in this book, it means *limited* monopoly. If you have played the board game Monopoly, you might work with the idea that a limited monopoly would be roughly comparable to owning two railroads out of three. In the United States I doubt the existence of any commercial monopolies that are not limited. Most of them are limited in scope. All of them are limited in duration.

In technology, monopoly is not a dirty word. In fact, the government, to encourage technological innovation, grants monopolies in the form of patents and (perhaps inadvertently, perhaps not) in the form of regulatory approvals (e.g., drug approvals by the Food and Drug Administration).

Absent government protection, a few companies build a wall around their business by doing something so incredibly difficult, intellectually, that it is a hard act for would-be competitors to follow.

Cisco Systems of Palo Alto is an example. They created a technology — a complex body of proprietary lore — that enables them to link otherwise incompatible computers. Many biotech firms and one or two banking software companies have also developed whole technologies in private, and thus enjoy substantial protection from competitive pressure. Some monopolies are built by steady, persistent marketing — by creating a wall of goodwill a brick at a time. (Medtronic, a company that has built its business selling pacemakers to cardiologists over a period of many decades, is not seriously at risk from competitive newcomers.)

If you see yourself as a long-term, buy-and-hold investor, the technology monopolies are the stocks to buy. If you are willing to both buy and sell stocks, then you can also profit by the short-term, Roman-candle success trajectory of companies that are not likely to achieve monopolies.

Finally, in the middle range are companies that have created a technology enabling their customers to break free from some other company's monopoly. This is how Apple and Compaq made their fortunes. They destroyed IBM's monopoly. Compaq was, for a time, the fastest-growing publicly held company in history. Such stocks must be held and watched closely for an intermediate period — several years — until they either create a monopoly of their own or exhaust the commercial energy (of restless captive customers) pent up over time by the monopoly under attack.

To buy technology stocks well, it is sometimes necessary to unlearn or shed some ingrained (and perhaps treasured) ideas about the qualities that should make a technology stock an attractive buy. These are mostly nineteenth-century ideas and ideals, the revered lessons of the industrial revolution.

For example, many investors believe that technical innovation is inherently a good thing; that it adds rather than subtracts value; that one original idea can change the world and make millions of dollars; and that good earnings growth is the signal of a stock on its way up. Most people tend to buy stocks they feel they can root for, and this often means, of course, that they buy the underdogs.

Just to give these comfortable patterns of thinking a good shake, it is helpful to consider the story of Compaq. At this company in its early stages, innovation was regarded as a potentially costly error and originality was not tolerable. Earnings growth was dismal by design. The company was never an underdog. It started at the top and went up from there.

If you had purchased $14,000 worth of Compaq at its 1984 low, instead of a car perhaps, you would have become a millionaire in this stock in late 1994. This means an averaged return of $100,000 per year for ten years. Fourteen grand well spent.

Compaq is not just a special case. For technology investors it should be studied as the classic case — almost a controlled scientific experiment. Compaq triumphed in a unique competition where the value of technological innovation was reduced to zero. Its story shows us what counts in a technology business when technology itself is factored out of the equation. What counts most heavily is gaining control of a network — a sales and distribution network, in this instance. Other lessons:

- When it appears that a technological field is "exploding," it usually means, at bottom, that *competition* in that field is exploding. In a gold rush, only a few fortunes are made.
- Earnings growth, which is supposed to be a good predictor of stock price appreciation, is actually a poor and unreliable indicator of future success in technology companies. It is not a bad inverse indicator, however, since Compaq's low was coincident with its least promising earnings reports.
- In any competition of par products, capital wins. Bigger is better. Balance-sheet strengths, such as big cash positions, cannot foreshadow victory, but weakly capitalized companies cannot win. Do not reflexively side with the underdogs. Their stocks are cheap but they tend to get even cheaper.

Compaq is an amazing case study in how to build a technology company around a wholly unprotected and apparently unprotectable idea. In 1982 this idea was lying on the ground, like a lost wallet, for anyone to pick up. It was the blueprint for the IBM personal computer, which was published (not to say broadcast) by IBM in its own technical manuals and references.

Around that time I visited the office of a computer logic designer who was using IBM's helpful reference books to contrive a clone of the IBM-PC. Gesturing with incredulity at the published circuits, logic diagrams, and specifications bountifully covering the top of his desk, he said, "Look at this. They really . . . IBM has spilled its guts, here. It's wide open."

He believed IBM had revealed its personal computer technology intentionally. Perhaps he was rationalizing product theft, and perhaps he was also correct. Apple's computers had succeeded in establishing a technical standard that software writers and aftermarket hardware manufacturers could adhere to in defining their own products. The technical standard, in turn, made Apple a standard.

By the early 1980s, the Apple II had already become the centerpiece of a new industry in which a diverse range of new products — chiefly software and circuit boards — appeared from many different manufacturers. All these products could be used without modification on an Apple; all proclaimed in common their "Apple compatibility." My logic designer friend speculated that perhaps IBM's purpose in making it so utterly easy for him to scrutinize and copy the technology of its new IBM-PC was to quickly establish a new, rival hardware standard to compete with Apple's.

This IBM did. Its personal computer achieved immediate acceptance. The PC was a huge seller. And by the late spring of 1983, more than 150 companies had gone into the business of manufacturing clones of the IBM-PC, all conforming to IBM's hardware and software standard. IBM seemed unperturbed by all the clones.

It was a famously unemotional company. Because it was IBM — *the* IBM — it could count on retaining an enormous share of market. Every one of the knockoffs claiming IBM-PC compatibility was in some sense an advertisement deferring to the original, the real thing, the IBM personal computer. Finally, maybe IBM viewed this sudden avalanche of cheap little boxes, the PCs, as terminals to be linked someday to its own big expensive boxes: the heroically scaled IBM mainframes it saw as the real computer business.

Anyway, it was as evident to IBM as it was to everyone else that 150 different IBM-compatible personal computers would not simultaneously fit on the shelf of any retail computer store. There would be a shakeout. There would be many losers.

When Compaq suddenly popped up with the formal launch of their new computer, at a splendidly orchestrated press conference at the Waldorf Astoria in November 1982, they were perhaps the 151st entrant in the IBM-PC clone derby. It was not at all clear they would win. The Compaq had a distinguishing quality — it was portable. Some other PC clones were also portable, so this was not a unique feature. Otherwise it was pure clone — Compaq urged that it was the purest clone of all.

The company had been formed by three former employees of Texas Instruments who had (the press duly reported) designed the Compaq computer prototype on a place mat after lunch in a Chinese restaurant on Jones Road in northwest Houston.

Texas Instruments did not blithely accept an exodus of Houston employees that followed the original trio to Compaq, and TI filed many lawsuits against Compaq's founders and early employees. In time, less and less was heard of these lawsuits in the trade press. An acquaintance of mine, drinking cold beer on a sultry Houston summer night, explained to me his personal take on these events. He cast himself in the role of a Texas Instruments corporate attorney, presenting what he saw as TI's case against Compaq to a Texas judge, as follows: "Your honor," he said, "these Compaq sumnbitches have stolen their computer from Texas Instruments before Texas Instruments could even *start* stealing it from IBM." Shifting roles to that of judge, my well-lit friend quickly found TI's case to be without merit.

My friend captured the tenor of the times, but he was wrong about the details. Texas Instruments did eventually unveil a personal computer, but it was not an IBM compatible. They sought to distinguish their computer in the traditional way by making it a better computer than IBM's. Technological innovation. Originality. Big mistake. In that curious first IBM-PC clone war of the early 1980s, no rewards would accrue to originality; rather, the winning quality was proved to be that of exactly-alikeness.

The crucial idea that a computer could be exactly like IBM's in every respect save price was a difficult one for clone makers to present or say out loud in so many words. Finally, the transparently coded expressions "100 percent compatibility" and "a work-alike" came to be understood as implying, though not quite meaning, a 100 percent knockoff. Voices were raised to question the many competing claims to 100 percent compatibility, for it seems that some compatibles were indeed created more compatible than others.

Strictly speaking, Compaq's designers did not copy the IBM-PC. They used unprotected technology in the same way IBM used it; and they invented circuitry and software as required, wherever IBM's proprietary rights were clearly established, to work their way around those rights. It would have been stupid — nihilistic — for Compaq or any other clone builder to create an exact replica, and so they did not.

Compaq's excellent engineers could help the newborn company avoid a pitfall in the patent courts, but avoiding defeat is not the same as engineering a victory. Victory in the IBM-compatible computer market could not be assured by engineering at all, since by definition all 150-odd competitors were striving to replicate all of the same product advantages — and disadvantages. They shared identically the same technology, as standardized to the published specifications of the IBM-PC.

No one except perhaps Texas Instruments really wanted to create a computer superior to IBM's. They all wanted to create a superior copy — superior, that is, to 150 other copies. So in this difficult, extremely counterintuitive business, Compaq secured its victory in a simple and direct way. They bought it.

Of the 150-plus original competitors I cannot, twelve years later, think of a single other survivor. Victor, Vector, Corona, Hyperion — where are they now? While these rivals were earnestly constructing their various machines, Compaq's management was building a war chest. Compaq's chairman and co-founder, Rod Canion, enlisted Ben Rosen, a former Morgan Stanley analyst now regarded, in retrospect, as one of the country's most perceptive (and richest) venture capitalists. With Rosen's help, Canion won for Compaq in just a few months the largest pool of venture capital that had ever concentrated on a single venture — $25 million up front.

Rod Canion is a careful, thoughtful, well-spoken, and quietly religious engineer, more in the mold of a chess player than a poker player. He was then in his early thirties. One might have expected him to act a bit tentatively — to husband or reserve the capital he had put together. Instead, he used it. He used it quickly and he used it brilliantly.

Because of its uniquely enormous capital base, Compaq was able to offer potential computer dealers solid reassurance about its future stability as a manufacturer and about the inherent manufacturing quality of its machine. Compaq was positioned as a BMW to IBM's Mercedes. Quality touches were evident because they were made to be evident. The structural chassis of the computer was aluminum, neatly perforated with lightening holes, anodized in gold. Critical electrical contact points were gold plated. The machine had a technically superior aesthetic, like a racing car or a rocket-borne instrument package.

Compaq also made it a point to set and maintain a wide, wide spread between its wholesale price to dealers and its "suggested retail price." Dealers, at their discretion, could use the spread either to offer deals to their customers or to enhance their profit margins.

The extremely handsome allowance for dealer margins assured a place of honor for Compaq's attractive new machines on the shelf next to the IBM-PC. The Compaq was a better deal for both dealer and customer. It was priced 20 percent below the IBM-PC standard and yet, thanks to the generous margin agreement, it could return a whopping profit to the dealer.

Academic question: Out of 150 PC-compatible computers, which one would a computer dealer, so generously favored by Compaq, be most likely to stock? Answer: Compaq. Asked for counsel on which computer to buy (technology being equal, retail prices being lower, margins being better), which computer would the dealer recommend to his retail customers? Compaq. This single, expensive tactic alone might have assured the company's success. But there was more.

They hired Ogilvy & Mather, arguably the best advertising agency around, and certainly the best one in Houston, Texas, at that time. They asked for help. Kirk Walden, who was Compaq's account manager at Ogilvy & Mather, presented the original advertising plan to Compaq's management. The thick formal plan, Walden recalls, was entitled *Get Famous Fast!*

The company spent $10 million to achieve this end in a single year, using television while 150 rivals were, Walden says, "mired in the trade magazines." At the end of the year, Ogilvy's tracking studies showed that Compaq had become the third most visible computer company in America, after IBM and Apple.

And, in its first year, Compaq enjoyed stellar revenue growth. From a standing start, its gross revenues shot to $111 million. The year after that, Compaq sales vaulted again, to $323 million. It was the fastest-growing company in history. Yet it was often and sternly criticized in the financial community. Analysts, insisting as they usually do on good and growing earnings per share, pointed out that Compaq's own profit margins were awfully slim. On each and every unit sale, it seems, the Compaq dealer kept a wolf's share of the money.

In the background, however, offstage right and left, the competition was committing suicide. The 150 competitors were decimated — they had no way to reach their customers. Their products were not stocked, not displayed, not sold. Bankruptcies ensued.

On their way to oblivion, and as their money ran out, some of these computer manufacturers issued common stock. Investors, eager to get in on ground-floor opportunities in this exciting (obviously exploding) high-technology field, bought the stocks eagerly. They did not do well by these investments.

Compaq stockholders also endured periods of deep stock price weakness. Because the company was not deemed profitable enough by analysts, and because of the destructive clone war then so visibly in progress (and because Compaq had taken on IBM, for heaven's sake, not to mention Texas Instruments), in late 1984 you could have purchased Compaq stock for a split-adjusted price of $0.58 per share.

This was, amazingly, a price somewhat lower than the company's liquidation value. In other words, if the company had stopped doing business, sent everyone home, and sold off its plants, inventory, and equipment, and then distributed the proceeds and its cash to its creditors and shareholders, the stock probably would have returned more than $0.67 per share. So this is how the stock market valued the fastest-growing company that ever was. Like dirt.

Few investors understood that profits were weak because the company was purchasing a huge share of market and a great victory. But then, at the midpoint of the decade, the analytical mists parted and the pie charts of the personal computer industry were suddenly, clearly, seen to be divided into three large segments — IBM, Apple, and Compaq. The few other survivors of this first great clone war were lumped together into that small pie segment invariably labeled "Others."

At about this time, Compaq's margins and earnings per share began to improve. It had not exactly created a monopoly — but one might say it had created a near monopoly in the business of breaking IBM's monopoly. What about the stock? Just three years past its 1984 low, it had rocketed up 200 percent. The case history ends here, although the stock more than tripled in value after that. The major players have left the stage, the story line has changed.

Compaq's successful original strategy was kept in place until a new generation of competitors figured out how to bypass the dealer network — Compaq's choke point on the business — and market directly to computer purchasers. Dell, Zeos, AST, Digital, and others have joined this renewed fray. There has followed a second great clone war, one that may yet put an end to the personal computer business as a business, or simply drop it into the laps of the semiconductor manufacturers.

There are many helpful stock-buying insights to be gained by studying the Compaq startup. Technical cleverness sometimes triumphs. David beat Goliath. But in a clone war, where standardization is everything and technical cleverness works against you, bet on marketing and money. Technology alone does not confer any advantage to a manufacturer. If it is unprotected or insufficiently protected by patents or trade secrets, then the technology-based product must be protected in some other way. Compaq protected the technology somebody else (IBM) had created and then, for whatever reason, left out on the sidewalk. Compaq adopted this orphan and then protected it by buying control of the means of distribution — the dealer network.

It often turns out that protection can be afforded by some sort of network. This is thematic in technology success stories, from CBS to AT&T, from the railway networks to broadcasting networks to power companies and cable TV nets. In the case of Compaq, the crucial network was of the simplest type. It was a sales-and-distribution network.

Compaq's flattening defeat of its competitors was foreordained — not by superior technology but by superior capitalization and marketing. They assured their own ultimate victory by launching the company with more money than anyone else in business had ever started out with. They did not squander it. They used money like muscle, to force the competition aside. They also had the propulsive force that accrues to any company that offers alternatives to products fielded by a monopoly — in this instance, IBM's.

Compaq was never the underdog. All the underdogs lost. Victory is expensive. It costs capital and it puts a drag on earnings growth. This accounted for Compaq's low stock price, and, in the company's most heroic hour, rendered it a very good buy indeed at $0.58 per share.

Technology fortunes typically are based on monopolies. When a technological monopoly begins to break down, as IBM's did, certain other companies can make fortunes on its demise. But not just any company. To invest in such stocks you need to follow some simple rules for identifying, from information freely available in the public domain, those companies most likely to benefit from monopoly making or breaking — and those merely fashionable wunderkinder fated for a very short season of success. Specific numbers and rules you may find helpful are presented in detail in chapter 22. But the important first step is learning the name of the game: it is Monopoly, of course.

Chapter 4

How Much to Pay: Pricing at the Golden Median

CONSIDER BUYING TECHNOLOGY STOCKS with price/earnings ratios in the neighborhood of 21, plus or minus 4 points. The centerline price/earnings ratio, 21, will slide up and down, and if it slides down a bit, so much the better. But 21 is a useful midrange value. Fine — but to begin at the beginning, what *is* the price/earnings ratio?

The price/earnings (P/E) ratio tells you how many dollars you must pay to purchase one dollar of a company's earnings. The P/E ratio is the yardstick most stock market players use to evaluate the price of a stock. The P/E is so well and widely recognized as a tool for valuing stocks that it is published every day in the stock tables of newspapers, adjacent to the volume, high, low, and closing prices. For most stock buyers, the P/E is the real price of the stock.

The quoted price is essentially a meaningless number. A stock certificate that costs $85 is not necessarily a more expensive piece of paper than a stock certificate that costs $1.

The $1 stock may well represent the assets of a company that is unprofitable. In this case you are purchasing a share of its losses. This is like buying a hole in your pocket. The $85 share may well return more on your investment than a $95 share of some other company's stock.

The problem here is that the term *price per share* insufficiently describes the product. What you are buying is not just a share certificate, not merely a piece of paper. You are buying assets and liabilities, gains or losses, alert management or passive caretakers, a promising future or a corporate doomsday. This is why most investors quickly skip past price per share and ask how much each share can earn for them.

Many experienced stock investors shop for a stock with a low price/earnings ratio, coupled with a low price/book value ratio. These low ratios are thought to mark a bargain-priced stock. In picking science-and-technology stocks, however, the method is not sufficient. If it is applied as a dogmatic principle, it is a clear prescription for failure.

The reasons are not at all obvious, but they are compelling. If you are going to invest in science-and-technology stocks, you may need to rethink your concept of what constitutes a "right" price. This is partly because the market has changed, and partly because society has changed.

Perhaps the most successful investment doctrine of the twentieth century was based on the principle of "value investing" as espoused by Benjamin Graham. It urged that stocks should be bought cheaply — very cheaply — at prices even below book value. (The book value of a company is its net worth, divided by the number of shares outstanding. Net worth is assets minus liabilities. Assets are things like cash and machinery. Cash certainly matters but machinery may not, as we shall see.)

The value-investing thesis is elaborated in a fine, thick book by Graham and Dodd, published by McGraw-Hill. It is virtually a canonical text on Wall Street and has formed the theoretical basis for great fortunes, most notably perhaps that of Warren Buffet, who knew and worked with Benjamin Graham. Investors are intuitively happy with the notion of buying assets cheap. It works at the grocery store; it ought to work on the stock market. In fact, it does work. It works especially well for mature industrial companies.

Curiously, if you strictly applied the principles of value investing to technology stocks, you'd almost never buy one. (Of course, you would have purchased Compaq near its low and retired on the proceeds, but it is rather an unusual circumstance, isn't it, when the fastest-growing company in the world drops below book value?) If you adhere to the value-investing premise you will only rarely profit from a technology stock — and it also follows that some other set of guidelines must be brought into play in evaluating science-and-technology companies.

Industrial wealth was produced by capital equipment — factory machinery, furnaces and forges, mills, presses, drills, and lathes. (Karl Marx liked to call these assets the *means of production*.) Naturally, if the stock market price of such wealth-producing assets should sink below liquidation value, that price would be logically bound to rise. Hence, according to this thesis, if you find such a deeply depressed industrial stock, you should buy it.

In a software company, however, wealth is not produced by using capital equipment to add value to some raw material. Wealth is instead produced by brains almost directly, in a process the Germans have called a "headbirth." The manufacturing process — the mechanical reproduction of a product that has been somehow winnowed out of human thought processes — makes an almost trivial contribution in terms of value added to a raw material. In other words, 99 percent of the value (profit, wealth) is added by the programmer — by thinking — and 1 percent by the technically easy and mindlessly repetitive act of magnetically replicating and packaging the program.

So there is no important relationship between the hard capital assets of a software company — that is, its machinery — and its power to produce wealth. It isn't a gold mining operation with buckets and belts and dredges. For a stock picker, searching a database of software companies for wealth-producing plants and equipment priced below liquidation value is a pointless exercise. You can find such stocks, but there is no reason to suppose they will rise higher than their book value. This is because the assets (desks, mice, desktop computers) do not produce wealth like machine tools. Brains do. The same is true of biotechnology companies, whose tangible assets also include mice, and rats as well. It is increasingly becoming true of electronic and computer companies.

Cash is an important asset, and you should look at it separately, as a direct measure of a technology company's survivability. For example, analysts sometimes rank the biotech companies in order of their "burn rate," that is, the rate at which they are burning through their cash. These companies are typically cash rich from stock offerings and have not yet produced a product for sale.

A burn rate ranking tells you a little something about these companies' relative future value — their chances — because it hints at who might run out of money first. If you rank these companies in terms of a simple price-to-book value ratio, however, you will learn much less about any one biotech company's future value. This is because the price-to-book ratio is calculated on a point reading of cash, today's cash, without regard to how rapidly it is draining away into salaries, overseas subsidiaries, and the like.

In summary, the price-to-book seems sort of antiquated as a tool for valuing science-and-technology stocks. If the ratio of price to book value cannot tell us the whole story, then what other measures should we use in valuing the stock? The price/earnings ratio alone? Let's consider it.

The P/E ratio is the most widely used yardstick for pricing stocks. It makes sense. If a company is profitable, its earnings will be large. What you must pay to obtain a share of this stream of earnings is expressed by the P/E ratio. For a high-priced stock, you might have to pay $20 for each $1 of company earnings; this represents a P/E ratio of 20. For a "cheap" stock, you might be able to buy the $1 of earnings for a little as $5. Perhaps a bargain.

But the idea that good value is signaled by a low P/E ratio doesn't work for science-and-technology stocks. Again, the reason is suggestive of a fairly recent change in the way wealth is created — created, that is, on the stock market.

Since 1985, the stock market, consisting as it does of ten thousand publicly traded stocks, has been proceeding under a microscope. Computers watch every move that is made by every stock every second. They scan for value all the time, instant by instant, from the opening of the market each day until its closing. What are the computers looking for? The emergence of values, of bargains.

Naturally, the judgment of the machines is programmed, and the programs' buy/sell criteria are strongly influenced by the P/E ratios of the stocks in view.

Now, the P/E ratio may or may not have been in past decades a fair signal of a bargain stock. Most analysts would agree that it provides, by itself, nothing but a good hint about the intrinsic value of a given stock. But because of the phalanx of computers that now constantly and restlessly scans the market, the P/E tells us as individual investors something new and quite different.

The P/E now tells us how *visible* a stock is to the ever-vigilant computers. To a computer, any stock with an extremely low or extremely high P/E will stick out like a sore thumb. For high P/E, read high visibility. And for low P/E, you must also read high visibility.

I rarely bother with a further analysis of a stock at either extreme. The computers and their masters will have long since analyzed them to a fare-thee-well, and they are certain to be fully priced at their present level. In short, a low P/E stock is likely to be cheap for some good reason. It is not a neglected or an (absurdly) overlooked bargain. Thanks to the computer revolution, the last "undervalued and overlooked bargain" probably vanished from the stock market, forever, around 1985.

If you are to discover a stock that is a real hidden bargain, you must look where the computers do not look. This is in the crowded middle of the pack, where P/E ratios are near the median value. This lesson, incidentally, will be familiar to devotees of detective and spy fiction. To lose himself, a character on the run must always melt into the crowd. To find him you must, as a first step, locate the crowd.

The median P/E ratio for science and technology ranges up and down between 14 and 27, depending on the temperature of the market. In a range bracketing today's median P/E — the "golden median" price range — the trick is to find a stock distinguished by something other than its P/E ratio. This usually means rapid revenue growth, monopoly potential, or superb technological promise — which is monopoly potential by another name.

If you must stray from the near-median price range, go straight to the higher-priced side. A high P/E technology stock is elevated because of rapid growth, and is quite likely to go higher. A low P/E technology stock is more likely to vanish.

A second, fundamental reason to ignore low P/E stocks is that science-and-technology companies are growth companies. People do not buy them because their earnings promise dividends at some distant future date. People buy these stocks because they zoom up. Instant gratification. A high P/E is normal for such stocks, and a low P/E is a danger signal.

New technology companies rarely pay dividends, and their present earnings are typically sacrificed to create growth by plowing back profits into the company. Refer to the case history of Compaq in chapter 3. For Compaq, subdued earnings reflected the high cost of buying — and locking up — a huge share of the desktop computer market. Weak earnings also made the stock appear expensive — yet poor early-earnings reports often prefigure skyrocketing stock prices.

Conversely, terrific earnings growth rates are rarely sustainable. They quite commonly carry their greatest promise just before the stock price tops — and turns south.

Price/earnings ratios are wildly inflated by tiny earnings in the denominator (numbers like a penny or two per share), and this is another good reason to attach limited importance to the P/E ratio valuations of technology stocks. An elevated P/E often makes them look a lot more expensive than they actually are.

You have perhaps noticed there is a school of business journalism that is difficult to distinguish from jeering. This style is frequently adopted in a standardized, recurring, set piece article about the high price of high-tech stocks. I have read this same, basically preformatted article many times over the years in many different papers. It seems to surface annually, like the "ten-worst-dressed" feature.

The article urges that shareholders and readers should be shocked and amazed to learn that XYZ-Cor or HootisTech or BioZot have P/E ratios of 2,000 and 347 and infinity, respectively. The writer invariably concludes that "the techs are getting frothy," that fools are rushing in, that the sky is about to fall, and so on in this vein. Perhaps this recurrent story appears when business news is slow; or when the writer has purchased an illicit short position in one of the supposedly overpriced stocks; or when the writer is naive or credulous enough to listen to the hissing whispers of short sellers on the phone.

A short position increases in value as a stock goes down. Some short sellers attempt to enhance the value of their positions by telephoning business-page journalists to inquire whether or not a certain stock has perhaps "come a little too far." According to *The Wall Street Journal* — which laudably published an exposé of this practice, and named names — short sellers often work in concert to spread skepticism, and they get the ball rolling by phoning journalists first. Technology stocks are favorite targets for short sellers — easy shots — because of their typically inflated P/E ratios.

Don't give short sellers a second thought. Short sellers affect prices, but only in the short term, sometimes for just a few days, during which they may focus their energies and resources on a particular stock. They can't just walk away from a short position — they must buy their way out of it. If the stock is sound, this buying will put it back where it started, usually abruptly. The reason to be aware of short sellers is to make sure they cannot panic you out of a long-term stock position by orchestrating a sharp but spurious price nose-dive.

A stock with a P/E ratio of 2,000 is not necessarily an overpriced stock. It is the ratio, not the stock, that has been overvalued. By definition, the P/E ratio is a pretty bizarre number. For earnings near zero, like a penny, the ratio begins to explode. For earnings at zero — a company whose business is at breakeven, which is not a terrible thing — the ratio does explode. It becomes infinite. Finally, as earnings degrade from breakeven to a one-penny loss, the P/E ratio goes from infinity to nonexistence. This is not how prices work in the grocery store, and one more reason I find it hard to justify using P/E as a direct plugin for price, as investors are commonly taught to do.

Here is how I suggest using it. First, write down the names and the P/E ratios of a big, generous handful of technology stocks, perhaps fifty or sixty, chosen at random. You can pick the stocks and their P/E ratios right out of the daily newspaper.

Next, make a simple graph. An example is shown in the accompanying figure. Scale the horizontal axis with numbers ranging from 10 to 70. Working from the top of your list of stocks, make a star on the chart corresponding to the P/E ratio of the first company. Then the second. Keep doing this boring, meticulous work. It is worth a great deal of money.

Soon you will notice that the stars are stacking up highest on top of some central P/E value, perhaps 18 or 20, but that only a few stars accumulate on top of higher P/E values, such as 36. Eventually the

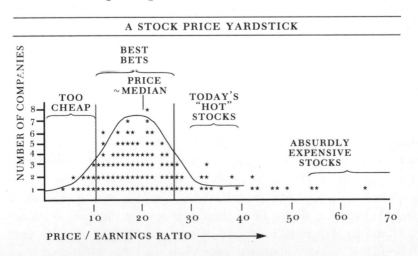

outline of a bell-shaped curve will emerge, as in the figure. The bell curve is a pricing map that shows you where you are. Armed with this simple, seemingly simplistic homemade diagram, you now have a clear view of what "high" and "low" technology stock prices really mean.

The median or centerline value is most important. In bear markets, it may sink as low as 14. If it does, buy some stocks.

In a runaway, hysterical bull market, the centerline price will flash as high as 34. This means that all technology stock prices are too high. It is a good sell signal.

When journalists exclaim over exalted technology stock prices, they usually quote an *averaged* P/E ratio: an utterly out-of-sight number like 40, 50, or 60, depending on the pool of stocks chosen to be included in the average. Such averages are meaningless because they are "pulled" so strongly by a few exceptionally high P/E stocks. In an averaging calculation, just one biotech stock with a P/E of 2,000 (a $20 stock with earnings of one penny per share) has the same weight in the calculation as *ten* other technology stocks, each with a P/E of 20. The arithmetic process of simple averaging produces a freakishly high P/E for the whole group. For this reason you should always rely only on median P/E values. Ignore averaged P/E values.

Notice from the diagram that the envelope of the bell-shaped curve dips to the horizontal axis at a point corresponding to a P/E ratio of 29. This 29 is a reasonable upper limit on the price you should pay for any technology stock on that particular day. Hidden values can probably be found near the centerline, plus or minus a few points.

Stocks whose stars appear above the 29 level are running ahead of the pack. Typically they are institutional darlings. Stocks such as Cisco, Microsoft, or Amgen have, each in their day, repeatedly turned up in this exceptionally high P/E range. This is how you can quickly pick out the "high flyers" of the current market. They are bid up, chiefly by mutual funds, because of their growth and (in a self-fulfilling system of success) because they are being bid up by mutual funds. It is okay to buy such stocks in a bull market. As the bell curve advances to the right, the leading stocks will advance even faster. But note that they are hardly undiscovered bargains, and keep your finger on the trigger. Don't buy unless you can sell quickly and decisively.

Finally, at the rightmost extreme of the chart are stocks that are not likely to stay there. They should be sold or shorted, or justified with some very special reason to buy, such as the patent rights to the world's first successful nuclear fusion reactor.

I use a computer to generate one of these pricing bell curves every day, but it is not necessary to use a computer for this task, nor even to check the graph frequently. Once each quarter is probably sufficient.

The bell curve is a big help, but it does not provide enough detail. The P/E ratio curve shows you clusters of stocks that *might* be attractive buys, and it definitely shows you which ones are too cheap, too visible, and too elevated in price to consider. But it does not show you which specific stocks are most attractive as buys. It does not, in other words, show you the "real" price of a technology stock.

What to use instead?

There are many other "price per" ratios. Price per cash flow, price per sales, price per earnings growth rate, price per cash. In my experience, a ratio based on price-per-percentage sales growth has proved to be the best initial guideline. Step-by-step valuation methods are presented in chapter 22 to help you determine when the price is right.

As a last consideration, let's drop all the ratios for a moment and return to the stock quote, the absolute price per share. In theory it means nothing. An $85 share might be vastly expensive or a great bargain, once the price has been re-expressed in terms of ratios like earnings per share or asset values per share. But that raw number, $85, is the psychological equivalent of an ice bath. A lot of investors will avoid jumping into it, no matter what the ratios say. Anything a lot of investors will do — or avoid doing — matters.

This is one reason stocks split. Arithmetically, a split has no effect at all but psychologically, shares seem more attractive to more people at lower absolute prices. Is there some scale of psychological price resistance? Of course, but it is subjective, not quantitative. I personally prefer to buy stocks priced between $8 and $35.

If an $8 stock gains $1, you've made 12.5 percent on your investment that day. If an $80 stock gains $1, that's fine too, but it's only a 1.25 percent appreciation. Because of the promise of percentages, low-priced stocks are a lot more fun to own. Absolute price may be meaningless in theory, but it matters in practice.

In pricing a technology stock, the basic idea is the same as it has always been — to buy cheap and sell dear. The change you need to make is in the way the "good value" inherent in a bargain is defined. The goodness is based more on rapid growth than on current earnings.

In a "discovery" stock, value arises from the obscurity that blankets all stocks in the crowded, boring middle of the P/E range — in the computers' blind spot. In plain numbers, this usually means a P/E in the neighborhood of 21, plus or minus 4 points. For a higher P/E stock, one that has already been discovered (discovered, that is, by the mutual funds and other institutional investors), value arises from a bandwagon effect: the well-established principle that nothing succeeds like success. One buys such stocks even though they are not intrinsically bargains, simply because they are going up.

Chapter 5

How to Distinguish Between the Stock and the Story

STOCKS OFTEN SEEM TO behave irrationally — good ones go down, bad ones go up. This chapter discusses the reasons why, and suggests ways to see past one's own frustration to what is really going on.

Consider this situation. A drug company has great sales growth, and earnings are beginning to burgeon. Debt is zero; there is a huge cash hoard. Patents and FDA approvals have locked in a monopoly product, which is a helpful and effective treatment for a chronic disease. Is this stock a buy?

Let's reserve judgment and look at a second company. This one has flat sales growth, a series of earnings reports that have profoundly disappointed analysts, big debts, and a sinking stock price. The product, a circuit board, has been successfully replicated in Singapore, and clones are being imported massively by rival companies. Should this stock be sold or shorted?

The answers seem altogether obvious in each case. But the obvious answers are not necessarily the right answers, in terms of your own stock market strategy, because the real question has not yet been asked. The real and crucial question is this: Are these facts visible to the market?

Bad news will not make a stock go down if it isn't really news, that is, if it is wholly predictable. Good things will not make a stock go up if they are wholly unsurprising. Any new fact you learn about a technology company must be evaluated — not on its face value but on the basis of whether the news is already "in the stock."

Most of the time, most of what you hear or read about a given company is indeed "in the stock." Most news is thoroughly discounted into the stock price long before you read it in *The Wall Street Journal* or hear about it on *CNBC* or *The Nightly Business Report.*

This is why the homily that "a good company will have a good stock" does not really reflect good sense. A company can be a very good one indeed — without being a good buy. As a rule, a good company will have high visibility and a fully and accurately priced stock. An accurately priced stock is not a bargain stock, because a bargain by definition is a stock priced below its real value. A failing company will also have high visibility and an accurately priced stock — but it is not really a bargain at any price north of its liquidation value.

The stock market is not exactly designed to keep secrets. As you read good and bad business news, in the quiet and privacy of your favorite chair, or perhaps perched in front of your computer screen, remind yourself occasionally that a few million other investors are simultaneously reading that same good and bad news — over your shoulder, as it were. Business news on TV is even more obviously broadcast to multitudes.

Experienced investors and professionals eye the news in a peculiar way. They are prepared to learn from it, but they are not much intrigued by the literal content of a news story. They understand that any fact about a stock they are hearing or reading has already been published or broadcast, and is therefore too well and widely known to trade upon.

What interests professionals is not the content of the news but the market's subsequent reaction to it. If the news about a specific company is bad, and it comes at the end of a long string of bad news, the market may not react at all. This unreaction would be read as a buy signal by many traders — an indication that everyone who might want to sell has already sold.

Say the news is good — perhaps a stellar earnings report. In a climbing stock the normal pattern of price reaction would be a quick runup followed immediately by a quick selloff. The whole pattern ratchets through the quote machines in a matter of minutes.

Day traders sell into the good news because they know that to-morrow will almost certainly fail to bring news as good as today's. Canny investors eye the stock closely in the week following this knee-jerk buy/sell sequence. If the stock's normal uptrend does not emerge in the week or ten days following good news, then it could well be that the pool of potential buyers is empty. This means the stock may have reached a major top, and would be a good candidate for sale.

Notice what's happening here. Instead of watching the news for direct clues on whether to buy or sell, professionals watch for the market's subsequent reaction or unreaction to news. Oddly, a lack of reaction in the market is the most significant signal for traders on both the buy side and the sell side. The most important, most dangerous, or most promising thing that can happen in the market is that *nothing* happens in the wake of a news or earnings report.

The traders' chosen word for this languid pattern of stock trading is *exhaustion.* They may say "the buyers are exhausted" or "the sellers are exhausted." What they mean is that the *supply* of buyers or sellers has been exhausted. The caricature image of a very tired stock buyer or seller is nevertheless a helpful mnemonic. Keep it in mind.

There is another, more quantitative way to regard good news and bad, and that is to use a computer to create rankings of technology stocks in order of their financial excellence or, perhaps, in order of their appeal as bargains. Such rankings are also frequently published in investors' newspapers, magazines, on-line stock services, and newsletters. These numbers and ratios reflecting financial strengths and growth rates are as much a part of a company's story as its marketing strategies, patents, and technical breakthroughs.

But you should never buy a stock from the top of such a list. As a first step, I usually discard the top fifteen companies in any published or computerized ranking. The reason is that these high-ranking companies are hovering near the top of every other analyst's computer screen. Because of their high visibility, they are most likely to be fully priced at their current price — not bargains.

You need not depend on the mass media (TV, newspapers, magazines, and computer networks) to bring you the news. You can get ahead of the news by using your own personal resources. The most direct way is to visit the companies you are interested in. If you really want to know how a business is doing, you can learn more by counting trucks at a loading dock than you can from weeks of studious attention to brokerages' analytical reports and corporate communiqués. If there are no trucks to count, well, that should tell you something too.

Students in graduate schools of business are presented with the concept of perfect information. The idea is that all available information about a company is instantly discounted by the stock market, so that the price of any stock at every moment is the right price. The notion calls to mind Wordsworth's quotable conclusion about the work of the Creator: "Whatever is, is right."

The concept of instantaneous stock price discounting is probably valid with respect to published information, but it breaks down completely if you try to apply it to trends and events happening in the real world in real time. A publicly held technology company I used to visit at intervals began to boom noticeably fully three months before the stock market registered any sort of reaction to its sudden new success.

The company popped from a deep loss to a handsome profit on the basis of a successful new product introduction — a fairly classical pattern of business recovery — but the stock didn't budge until after the appearance of that quarter's formal earnings report. So you can still profit in stocks just by keeping your eyes open.

Information about stocks is indeed distributed at the speed of light — once it gets into the information system. But there is a distinct lag between the occurrence of an event and the reporting of that event. If the significant change is a *trend* rather than an event — an uptrend or downtrend in business activity — there may well be no report of it at all until it is finally sampled and quantified, either as an industry statistic or as a quarterly earnings figure. The stock market, like the news media, is quick to pick up on occasions and events, but it is sluggish or uncomprehending when it comes to trends. You can use this to your advantage by ignoring events and scanning for trends. Sometimes you can identify a trend just by thinking things through. Sitting and thinking is a stratagem that rarely occurs to many market players, but it is surely the best one.

The market also takes a long time to digest comparative data. This is probably the biggest hole in the supposedly instantaneous stock market information system, and it is one where informed individuals can profit readily. Suppose a high-profile software company like Microsoft reports earnings today. The stock will react in a matter of microseconds to any deviation between actual earnings and those anticipated by analysts. Business reporters will duly report that the market has been favorably "surprised" if the stock pops up, or "disappointed" if the stock goes down. In other words, the actual reported result is evaluated, by the market mechanism, in terms of whether the company has measured up to research analysts' expectations.

This creates the impression that if you knew in advance, from published estimates, what the market's earnings expectations were for Microsoft — and then hurriedly measured the difference between the actual and the expected results at the very moment Microsoft published those results — then you, too, could rack up a quick profit on the market's surprises and disappointments. Forget it.

You can easily learn what earnings the market expects to see by checking the Zacks consensus of earnings estimates. You can do this with any computer. Use Telescan software as described in chapter 22. It is certainly helpful to review earning projections if you are following or considering a stock for the longer term. But you cannot expect to trade on earnings disappointments or surprises. The price moves too fast.

So how do you win?

Let's say Microsoft reports earnings on Monday, Netscape reports on Tuesday, and Oracle Systems reports on Friday. (This is realistic. Technology sectors tend to report earnings in clusters, and these are all software companies.) Throughout the following week, a spate of semiconductor and computer companies report earnings. At the end of this period you are in a position to make comparative judgments. You may notice which software company did the best job of controlling costs this quarter — and which one grew the fastest. You may also notice that margins are shrinking in the whole semiconductor group, yet profits are up and coming in the computer manufacturing sector. Comparative observations like these, made between companies and especially between groups of companies, will produce information for you that is only rather slowly reflected in the prices of stocks. In other words, it produces information that is early, unseen, special — and worth money.

Notice that the pricing machinery of the market focuses on each company in isolation. A simple mathematical model is made of the company by its analysts, and expectations are formed. (Great expectations? You bet.) Then the company reports its real results. The stock pops up or down in proportion as the company's earnings report "surprises" or "disappoints" its analysts, and that's that. The model is re-jiggered later in the day to reflect the new reality, and the market prances on to the next company in line to report earnings. Only one comparison has been made here, between a real company and a mathematical model of that company. It is an abstract, ingrown, and unworldly process.

It takes as much as six weeks for the market to begin making comparative measurements — to put individual companies into context by noticing how they did relative to their competitors and how they, along with their competitors, have done relative to companies in other stock sectors. Within this lag period, six weeks, you can buy low or sell high.

The vaunted, expensive electronic information systems that feed the markets must first be fed themselves. Numerical information as reported over the wire (i.e., the Dow Jones news wire), on the day it is reported, is considered by many market professionals to be too quick and dirty to be very useful in comparing companies and their stocks. This is because different companies follow different accounting procedures and practices. The typical six-week lag ensues while incoming data are adjusted by the information services. Their work assures comparability in numbers such as inventories, for which accounting practices may vary widely.

Value is added to the as-reported data by teams of accounting professionals, who clean it up and adjust it to a set of common standards. The finished product, a neat and nifty database permitting realistic comparative rankings of diverse companies (the stock market's equivalent of the Top Forty countdown), is then broadcast at last over the financial data networks. It is served at the speed of light, certainly, but it is very stale stuff indeed by the time it appears on the computer screens' menus. And who reads it? Who might comment upon it in the mass media?

Not analysts. Brokerage analysts are assigned to a specific company or to a group of similar companies within an industry group. They are specialists. A software stock specialist typically has little interest in comparing the results of his own group to that of, say, the biotech or pharmaceutical stocks. In fact, at most brokerages there is no person whose job it is to compare, let alone comment upon, dissimilar stocks.

Money managers must make such comparisons every day because dissimilar stocks are competing for their incoming cash. But most money managers, unlike analysts and brokers (who are paid to talk), are habitually and professionally cagey about what they say to the press. To them, a good investment idea is an unplayed card. They won't talk about it until they have made their play. Then they might talk — as still more time elapses.

So here is a nice little window of opportunity. You can use the quick-and-dirty data that become widely available as they are reported to create your own Top Forty. The procedure is slightly risky because the early data are indeed impure, at least in the purview of accountants, but you can learn to work with this, and the reward outweighs the risk. Chapter 22 provides specific procedures, but the main idea is simply that the market is slow to recognize and price-in facts that are based on making comparisons.

Maybe company A had a favorable earnings surprise, and the stock popped up. But within a week it becomes clear that its competitor, company B, has completely outclassed the whole group in terms of revenue growth. Company A perhaps improved its earnings by laying off employees; this turns out to be because company B is devouring the business. A is a sell, B is a buy. The market will be slow to catch on, because making this discovery requires a comparison between two or more alternative and sometimes dissimilar investments. You can learn to make such comparative judgments early and clearly. Perhaps the moral is this: when you are ready to buy a stock, don't base your decision on any single company's performance, viewed in isolation. Compare each candidate stock to every other stock on the market. This is not merely because it is a virtuous procedure, but because most market players have been slow to try it. They prefer to specialize. In specializing they ignore information — comparative information — that you can use to spot bargains.

Every stock has a story. A technology company, whatever its provenance, whatever its real story might be, will find its script rewritten as it is prepared (groomed, by its lead underwriter) to go public. When the company's stock is brought to market its founder must, it seems, come blinking onto the public stage as the typecast Thomas Edison character in our universal technology success story. Sometimes a dynamic duo is called for, like that of Hewlett and Packard or Wozniak and Jobs. Technology success is an American legend that has been retold thousands of times since the nineteenth century, with only slight thematic variations. The story is so familiar, in fact, that the audience notices and is entertained chiefly by the subtle departures from the great standard plotline.

The story must incorporate certain basic elements. For example: ". . . a guy went out to his garage one night and started banging on this piece of metal — an old tablespoon. First thing you know . . . patented the darned thing . . . everything from rocket motors to washing machines . . . market value already estimated at $250 million. . . . Government couldn't wait to buy it . . . 95 percent more efficient . . . ground-floor opportunity."

The legend is sustained because it is such a helpful sales tool. The seller of the stock — initially its underwriter, and in subsequent resales perhaps your own broker — tells the story because it is involving. You are supposed to read yourself into it. You are supposed to see yourself starting out small, coming up with a good idea, and growing big. It's as though your mother were telling you once again about Abe Lincoln's log-cabin origins and subsequent rise to the presidency — you are supposed to imagine yourself making a parallel climb to the top. Only it isn't your mother telling you the technology stock story — it is your broker, and your broker is, unlike your mother, self-interested.

It seems to be implied in this story's telling that when you buy the stock, you will be directly helping out the inventor or developer of the process or product that the company is founded on, as though he were perhaps your smart brother-in-law.

This is never true, and a good first step in distinguishing between the stock and the story is to recall this seldom-mentioned fact: the company does not actually get the money from your investment when you buy a stock. The cash you pay for the stock never reaches the company's coffers. Most investors are perfectly aware of this, but they don't think about it much, and maybe they just sort of forget it.

A company gets all its money from a stock offering up front, in the form of an enormous check from the underwriter of its stock. When you buy a stock, your own money goes to the person who sold it to you, not to the company. Most of the time, this means your money goes to a market maker, a professional middleman who maintains an inventory of the stock you have bought. Perhaps the shares you purchased from him were purchased by him, a few minutes earlier, for less money, from a former shareholder who was as eager to get out of the stock as you were to get into it. Notice that there is a little distance opening up here between the stock and the company.

The stock is a piece of paper traded on the open market. It represents a claim on the assets of the company. But buying that claim is not quite the same as passing your money directly, with a handshake, to the company's entrepreneurial president, the man or woman whose work you are complimenting by purchasing the stock. He or she will never see your money.

We are all natural partisans. We like to root for our stocks, and for the companies and people they represent. But the stock and the company are two different things. The company is real. The stock is an abstraction. The stock trades on the open market, and its price changes due to matters over which the company has little or no control — such as mass hysteria. What happens to the company does not necessarily happen to the stock. If the company does well, and there is a glut of stock on the market for whatever reason, the stock will not do well. If the company does poorly and it comes as no surprise to the market, the stock may suddenly shoot up on short covering purchases made by panicky short sellers. The company goes one way, the stock goes the other.

The stock and its story are linked, but only in indistinct or rubbery ways. We are often encouraged to believe that over time, the price of a stock must come to reflect the underlying value of the company, like a pendulum slowly coming to rest. I have never seen this happen, although perhaps it does. But in the near term (and we all live and work and make our investment decisions in the near term, which is to say, right now) the linkage is not mechanically positive and direct. It is as though the stock and the underlying company were tied together with a stringy pink material that is sometimes resilient and sometimes pops or snaps, such as bubble gum or Silly Putty.

Some investors — a great body of them, called technical traders — take the view that there is no useful relationship at all between the company's story and its stock. This means that the real world in which the company does business has nothing to tell us about how to profit in the trading environment in which the stock moves up and down. Technical traders generally take the view that any and all incoming real-world information is "already in the stock," that is, fully anticipated by and reflected in its price at the present moment. Strictly fundamental traders take a nearly opposite view, which is that the story is far more important than the stock. In this view an earnings report matters because the future growth it implies will "ultimately" be reflected in the price of the stock.

I regard both fundamental and technical market players as large clusters of real people — investors who have the power to move my stocks, whose behavior is more or less predictable from their two distinct and vigorously voiced ideologies. It does not seem to matter which group is "right" — you should take both points of view into account. Fundamental investors usually make money over time, but must endure losses and setbacks in the short term. Technical investors make a lot of money very quickly, but they typically lose it back over time.

I do think it is wise to mentally separate the company's story from the company's stock, something technical traders learn to do automatically. The stock and the company are subject to different market forces and often go in opposite directions because they trade in different markets. The company is immersed in the market for its own products, where it competes against other, similar products for its customers' sales dollars. The stock, in contrast, is immersed in the stock market, and competes against completely dissimilar stocks for investment dollars.

This produces some surrealistic contrasts and juxtapositions. A stock in a company that makes and sells silicon wafers must compete for your investment dollar against a stock in a company that makes and sells vanilla wafers. Maybe semiconductors are selling briskly this week, but the vanilla trees have been damaged by a typhoon. Money in the stock market will tend to flow from silicon wafers to vanilla wafers as the vanilla supply contracts, cookie prices skyrocket, and semiconductor investors scratch their heads. Perhaps these events develop logically, but the logic is never quite clear to anyone. For the semiconductor maker, the story is that business got better. The stock went down because investable cash went somewhere else altogether. Stock and story diverge.

It is psychologically helpful to simply view the stock as a thing entirely separate from the company. This way you can continue to admire the company as you coolly sell the stock — or buy a stock when the known facts about the company make it appear wholly unpromising. To succeed brilliantly at this game, investors and traders must sometimes make these difficult, counterintuitive moves. It's easier if you keep the stock in a mental compartment separate from that in which you keep and perhaps treasure the company's legend.

Some of the best science-and-technology stocks are those whose story has not yet been widely told. Technology companies that are not very newsworthy are most likely to be bargains. Since such stocks emerge from the middle of the pack, that's where you must look for them. They will be distinguished there, not by news or by a "good story," but by interesting, promising financial performance (chiefly rapid early sales growth and acceptable but slender current earnings) and by technology.

Distinguished by advanced technology? Rarely. The more "advanced" the technology, the further it probably is from realization as a commercial product. Look for a technology product for which there is a strong and obvious market; and for a technology that has the peculiar power either to make or break a monopoly. These are typically technologies associated with some sort of network.

Chapter 6

How to Avoid the Most Common Mistakes

THIS CHAPTER IS WRITTEN TO BE READ in bits and pieces, rather than all at once. This is because the subject matter — pitfalls, blunders, and errors of judgment — is so relentlessly negative. You may prefer to skip ahead to some of the fun, upbeat chapters on how to pick winning stocks. But bear in mind that in stock picking, getting it right is chiefly a matter of not getting it wrong. The stock market is a negative game, like golf. You start with a perfect score — zero — and with each stroke you take, the effort is counted against you. To win, you must make each stroke count. There is no allowance made for wasted motion or pointless flailing about.

In investing in science and technology, the things you *don't* do are far more important than the things you do. Investing is not a daily routine. It consists of making a very few precise purchases and sales, maybe twenty-five or thirty quickly accomplished transactions altogether in the course of a decade. A helpful corollary rule is that most of the time, the most intelligent course of action in managing stocks and funds is to take no action at all — yet it is not a passive pursuit.

The best strategy consists of energetically hurling aside the thousands of stocks and funds you don't need to buy, and avoiding the potential mistakes that may be urged upon you by the excitement of the market or the persuasive powers of stock and fund sales forces. The best way to guard against making mistakes is to learn to recognize and type them in advance.

Big mistakes are alarmingly easy to make in the stock market because things are so often the exact opposite of what they seem. Winners are often losers in the act of becoming. Bad news must often be received and understood as good news. And popularity for a stock may simply mark it as a target.

The single most common mistake is perhaps that treated in chapter 5. It is the mistaken idea that obvious, widely published information about a stock — that stock's story, good or bad — has somehow escaped the attention of the stock market and still has the power to influence that stock's price. It just doesn't.

Here is a brief guide to some of the other major fumbles of technology investing. You cannot avoid making mistakes in the market. Stocks go up and down, and mistakes are part of the cost of playing the game. But you can hope to avoid most of the really obvious, unnecessary, dumbbell mistakes — and in the stock market, an unmade mistake is the same thing as investable capital.

Suppose that an investor were hurried or perhaps hectored into the purchase of a stock that could easily have been recognized and typed in advance as a sinker. Over time, the stock and the investor's money will probably come back — but in the meantime, the investment is dead money. While the stock is down the loss is measurable both directly, as an unrealized loss, and in terms of money that could have done much better had it been invested later, or in stocks that were upward bound.

Purchasing last year's winner

This is one of a broad class of investment errors based on mistaking an event for a trend. Another example might be buying a stock on the news that it has just set a new high. The new high is an event — it does not necessarily point to a trend, such as a forthcoming series of new highs. More likely, it suggests a top.

The year's winners are duly announced by the media each January in virtually every category of human endeavor — in science, in film, in politics, in the selection of clothes to wear, and in stocks and funds. Logically speaking, this is just an annual ritual. The stock market does not somehow reset to zero at midnight on December 31. The first trading day of the new year is not different in kind from that year's midpoint day, or Boxing Day, or any other day at all. Yet the turn of the year has psychological power, and it has a clear impact on the financial-service businesses. Money moves. January in the money business is like the Christmas season in the retailing business. Much of the year's business activity is concentrated in this one gigantic month.

It is not difficult to see why. Everyone does a mental summing-up at the year's end, and resolves to do much better next year. Investments that have not performed well are dumped into the tax-loss selling period around Christmas. Liberated cash rolls back into the market through January, seeking better opportunities. Perhaps it is not surprising that some of this loose money flows to the tippy top of *The New York Times* or *The Wall Street Journal*'s lists of winning stocks and funds from the preceding year. Oh, yes, aha, the browsing investor muses. Number one. Up +234% in the year. *That's* the one we want.

Out of curiosity, I once created a computer program to track the gains and losses of one year's top ten science-and-technology stocks during the subsequent new year's first three months. Only two stocks eked out slight gains in this hangover period. Eight crashed. These results hint at odds favoring disaster of about four to one, with the one favorable outcome being a flat performance.

It is a statistical expectation that "everything regresses to the mean." What this suggests in a practical way, in stocks as in competitive sports, is that an exceptional gainer in one time period will likely retreat from the pinnacle in the next. Once you get to the top, there's nowhere to go but down.

If the time period in question happens to be the calendar year, a stock's odds for getting clobbered are much enhanced. This is precisely because the year-end winners are so heavily publicized. They become magnets for the money of naive investors. Short sellers know this, and they know how to profit by it.

In the first few days of the new year, last year's winners are pushed by massive publicity into a last, sudden, spasmodic runup in price. The instant they falter — a signal that the last buyer on the planet has now indeed bought — short sellers begin selling them down. Down they go with a vengeance. There is no difficulty in finding these stocks to short — there they are in the newspaper, the year's Top Ten.

Overlaid on predatory short selling is selling by investors who have achieved the gains noted in the paper, and have probably been eyeing them, uneasily, for months. Their reasoning is: if we can only hang on until January, we can take this obscene profit in the next taxable year, and thereby postpone the taxes on it. In other words, there is a second tax selling season for winners, in January, and it is likely to affect the top ten stocks most powerfully.

Add together short selling, deferred tax selling, a normal statistical regression effect, and the unrealistic year-end success fantasy created by the media's top stock rankings, and it is not hard to see why these "winners" so typically go straight down a well. The way to avoid this plunge is simple. Buy no stocks in January.

There are some points aside that you might find helpful. For example, suppose you find yourself holding a 234 percent gainer, but in some unexceptional month, such as September. If there is no particular reason to sell other than your mountainous winnings, then hold the stock through late December. Take the profit just after Christmas, pay the tax, and avoid the nightmare of watching your gains evaporate after your stock is named one of the year's ten best.

Everybody's getting in

This is an old saw. If everybody's getting in you should be getting out or getting short. The assertion that everybody's getting in is most likely to be heard from persons who have already gotten in. If the stock tip is so widespread that this famous cliché is being voiced, and you hear it, you can assume that no one who is saying it will buy the stock. They've already bought it. Who, then, is left among us who has *not* bought the stock? If you haven't, don't. Even if it were true that everyone is getting in, it would be a mistake to join the buyers. The idea is not to join a crowd, a mass movement, a gold rush. Rather, the idea is to anticipate a gold rush and to get in early, as a discoverer.

That stock will never come back

Technology stocks have surprising resilience. The newer ones are extremely volatile, meaning that they may swing to wild extremes — up and down — around their centerline. I have in mind a voice-processing company called Octel. I bought their stock at $26 and sold a few months later at $20 because I convinced myself it would never come back. It sank below $8 but in less than a year it came all the way back. It went on to make substantial gains. More typically, a bad downswing for a technology stock will take it down 27 percent. This is about 12 percent deeper than most investors (who often use a 15 percent decline as a stop loss) are willing to tolerate. In science-and-technology stocks, because of their unusual volatility, one should be prepared to pick and stick.

Making other people's mistakes

There is a great deal of free information available about stocks. It is distributed by brokerages, by PR firms, by pundits and journalists, and by the investor relations departments of companies whose stocks are publicly traded. So much free information is so freely available, in fact, that it does not seem to occur to people to look the gift horse in the mouth.

Do it. Market experts on television, for example, do not necessarily proffer the names of their three favorite stocks as an altruistic service to viewers. They may name these particular stocks because they, the experts, are wholly stuck in these favorite stocks, trapped, and they want them to go up. If you and other viewers, in their millions, respond by buying these stocks, then the experts have successfully peddled their problems. Do your own research work. Free advice isn't.

Misreading analysts

In a rising market, deeply detailed research reports of a good securities analyst can be a tremendous help. In a down market, analytical opinion is also helpful — but in a contrarian way.

Like the rest of us, analysts hate to be wrong. By the time a sinking stock exhausts the patience, credulity, and fidelity of an analyst (who in the act of selling is usually admitting that he or she made a mistake in recommending the stock in the first place), it will have been sold long since by just about everyone else in the world.

Thus, when an analyst finally says to sell, it is a good sign that the last of the selling pressure has been exhausted. Analysts seldom use the scare word *sell*. An analyst's "hold" recommendation, in the grotesque, encoded language of this business, is understood by the stock market as a "sell" recommendation. In a depressed market, I think the issuance of a "hold" is a dynamite buy signal. I have long toyed with the idea of launching a mutual fund called the Buy-on-Hold Fund.

Brokerage analysts have strong voices — voices multiplied by the platoons of brokers who (sometimes reluctantly, but dutifully) convey by repetition the analysts' views and recommendations to their own customers. There is a discounting mechanism at work here. The first customer to learn of an analyst's fresh buy or sell recommendation on a stock is, not surprisingly, the best customer. Brokerages' best customers are institutional investors who can move many millions of dollars in and out of the market. By the time the news percolates out through, say, six thousand retail brokers to their individual customers — that is, to private investors — the analytical pronouncement from the main office has already (long since) changed the price of the stock about as much as it is going to change.

Day traders sometimes seek to take advantage of the sudden runup caused by a major analyst's buy recommendation (or sudden selloff on a sell alert) by trading *against* the recommendation. The traders know that if the recommendation has been heard at all — that is, if *they* have heard it — then it is too late to try to follow it. Whatever potential interest may have existed in buying or selling the stock has been mined out by the vigorous sales calls of the institutional and retail brokers.

Analysts are widely believed to be obsessed with earnings, and to some extent they are. Interestingly, poor earnings are often the flip side of good revenue growth in a young science-and-technology company. The earnings draw sneers, the growth is ignored, and the stock fails to gain analytical favor.

Compaq Computer, the classic example, was so out of favor with analysts that at one point, while the company was expanding at the speed of a meteor shower, its stock price actually dropped below its book value. If you focus your own attention on something other than company earnings, such as revenue growth, you will find that conventional analytical opinion opens up bargains for you in technology growth stocks again and again. But you must be willing to invest against the consensus of analysts' recommendations.

Experts are at least as likely as anyone else to be right, and their opinions are always well founded on facts and research. The source and quality of analytical opinion is not in question. The method by which that opinion is distributed, via the brokerage sale networks, causes the value of an analyst's opinion to quickly degrade as the brokers work the phones and the stock price adjusts. By the time the median private investor finally gets the story, it has been transformed by too much telling into rather bad advice.

Buying new issues

It is rarely a good idea to buy into the initial public stock offering (IPO) of a science-and-technology company. New stocks follow a hairpin trajectory, and few traders have the gunfighter reflexes it takes to get out anywhere near the top. If you happen to want the stock, wait until it has been on the market awhile. A venture capitalist acquaintance suggests at least one and one-half years as a realistic waiting period. I use two to three years. By that time the stock has usually been oversold by the disgusted and disgruntled early takers, and the speculators are gone, and you can edge in at a pretty fair price.

A stock offering is like the launching of a ship. Special equipment and rigging is put in place to support the effort. To put it a bit less obliquely, the underwriter can support the price of the stock in the early going by buying it. A positive change in the price of a stock is its own advertisement. If a stock pops up $5 on its day of issue, this is noticed and, often enough, draws in new purchasers. A typical IPO gains about 11 percent over its offering price on the first day of trading. At the end of its first week it has usually held onto this gain, but after that it starts nosing down.

Since speculators on both the long and short side are well aware of the game in progress, new issues tend to buzz and vibrate for a few exciting days. Eventually, however, the stock must float on its own. The scaffolding and rigging of the launch scene are all too soon dismantled and stored. Buying support shifts to the next new issue. The speculators take their profits and leave, the publicity dies down, the public's interest dies down, and the stock price, as you might expect, dies down.

Consider the paper that has been marketed here. The typical new issue in science and technology is usually represented as a ground-floor opportunity. It never is.

The "ground floor" is where the venture capitalist got in. His basis in the stock may be as tiny as a few pennies. At the public offering, the stock may "come" at, say, $12. Calculation of the percentage gain to the venture capitalists — on the basis of the public offering alone, and leaving aside all other activities of the corporation, such as the actual doing of actual business — will be left as an exercise for the reader.

In advance of an offering, a stock prospectus is circulated. This is an extremely formal legal document that is published to meet the SEC's requirement for full disclosure. If you hold one in your hand, it is hard not to imagine that you have been *chosen*, favored with something private and special — a legal instrument — and that you are indeed being let in on the ground floor.

Look it over. If the prospectus describes a company that has done business for several years and is now seeking an equity investment from the public, then the prospectus will contain some basic financial history. This will tell you if the company is profitable and growing. If so, you might file the prospectus and consider buying the stock in the depressed aftermath of the public offering. But if the prospectus describes a new company with little or no operating history, throw it away.

A lot of new issues are simply too new. Like a new-model car, they are likely to have some bugs in them. It makes better sense to choose your stocks from among those with an established history of financial results, of trial and triumph and tribulation, as disclosed in the normal course of reporting over many quarters as a public company. As an investor, you can select from among thousands of such companies. Why forgo this important advantage to buy a stock about which you have little or no historical information?

You should not. If you buy an IPO, you are speculating, not investing. The rules of this special market are a little too *laissez* to be fair. If you like the stock, let it come public and allow two years for it to detoxify. Then see what you think. If you are going to buy one anyway, there is some reassurance to be gained by picking one with a reputable lead underwriter. In science and technology, I tend to favor offerings that emerge from Alex Brown, Hambrecht & Quist, Robertson Stephens, and Montgomery Securities.

Paying too much for a stock or fund

If you buy stocks, use a discount broker. Among discount brokers, choose one that really is one — some discount houses charge only slightly lower commissions than full-service brokerages. Shop. Request commission cards and compare them. For the most realistic assessment of comparative commissions costs, you need to determine various brokerages' commissions for specific transactions. If you have an Apple and $15, you can obtain from Heizer Software in Pleasant Hill, California, a handy little commission reporting program that compares the discount commissions costs you would be expected to pay on specific transactions (e.g., 100 shares at $35 per). The program was written by Donald Snelgrove, an investor and an F-16 pilot who has a pilot's characteristic interest in precision.

Don't sign up to pay a wrap fee. If you choose to buy a mutual fund, don't select one that has a front-end load (commission) or charges you any sort of penalty or fee for early redemption.

Falling in love

Don't. Any technology stock that has made substantial gains for you (+50 percent or more) is a candidate for sale. Learn to distinguish between tech stocks with short-, intermediate-, and long-term potential. The short-term stocks may have just one season in the market, a single runup, and you should sell such stocks on a hair trigger. Never take delivery of stock certificates — leave your stocks "in street name." This is a psychological aid to good selling. It's easier to sell when all you need do is pick up the phone and call your broker. In general, you will not need to sell very often, but when the time comes you must sell without hesitation or dithering. The decision can be made numerically by following methods outlined in chapter 23.

Chapter 7

How Many Science-and-Technology Stocks Should You Own?

SIXTEEN.

The purpose of owning many stocks, rather than one, is the well-recognized value of diversification in reducing risk.

Few market players are aware, however, that the value of diversification has a sharply defined limit. Textbooks on portfolio analysis suggest that for industrial stocks, the limiting value of diversification can be reached with just eight stocks. A portfolio containing only this small handful of stocks can have essentially the same risk as the S&P 500 — the whole market — and that is the maximum risk reduction that can be achieved by diversifying. If you bought all five hundred stocks comprising the S&P 500, your risk would be only marginally less than that associated with only eight stocks.

It is a mistake to buy more. This is because further purchases cut down the performance that can be brought to your portfolio by a few really strong stocks — runaway successes. Think about it. A 200-percent winner in a portfolio of fifty stocks will be simply averaged in with a pool of forty-nine relative dullards, and will have little power to elevate the performance of such a fat and sluggish portfolio. But in a portfolio of eight stocks, a substantial gainer will have a real impact at the bottom line.

This is not just theory. A typical experience with portfolios of science-and-technology stocks is that just two or three stocks will run away with the portfolio, scoring eye-popping gains month after month, pulling the whole portfolio up by its bootstraps. Naturally, it would be more delightful to own the two or three hot stocks and no others, since the rest of the stocks are basically going along for the ride, and act as a dragging anchor on the averaged performance.

Unfortunately, to cast a net broad enough to capture those two or three hot stocks, it is necessary to buy many more. No person, method, or machine can pick winning stocks with rifleshot accuracy. To put the odds on your side, you must fire a shotgun.

It is fine to own a few stocks if you plan to continue to accumulate stocks over time, and commit only a metered fraction of your capital to each stock. But if you own just two or three technology stocks because you wish to concentrate your resources — to make, in effect, one whopping roll of the dice — then you are making one of those famous dumbbell mistakes. Spread your risk. Cast a wider net.

It is well understood that you should not put all your eggs in one basket, but it is news to many investors that there is such a thing as too many baskets. This is a problem inherent in mutual fund investing, and the first step to solving it is to understand that it exists. If you buy an open-end mutual fund at all, you are probably buying too many stocks. The difficulty is that the year's hot performing stocks are averaged into a pool of, say, two or three hundred much more ordinary stocks, so that the fund's performance (and your own gain) is not much uplifted by the few big winners. Huge funds can bring to bear techniques that overpower this problem — basically, they can buy their way past it — but such techniques cannot work indefinitely. In general, the smaller the fund, the better it will do in the science-and-technology sectors.

In the real world, the one or two stocks that turn into runaway successes will account for each good year's performance. The best hope for the rest of the stocks is that they don't do too badly. In constructing stock portfolios I use sixteen stocks instead of eight because technology stocks are riskier than the industrials on which the textbook studies were based. It is not possible to say they are twice as risky — I doubt it — but I doubled the textbook value in the same spirit with which an engineer doubles the calculated minimum strength required of a bridge. It creates a margin of safety on the risk side, and it casts a somewhat broader net than an eight-stock portfolio. Experience over the years with real portfolios of science-and-technology stocks under management at the Princeton Portfolios suggests that sixteen-stock portfolios have indeed performed better than eight-stock portfolios.

What about stock allocation? What is the best mix of asset types?

Occasionally — perhaps once each quarter — an ideal asset allocation plan is nailed up (usually by a brokerage), declaring that everyone should be positioned, say, 30 percent in long bonds, 10 percent in cash, and 60 percent in common stocks. This is always interesting but useless information. The correct asset mix for you is unique to you. It must take into account your risk tolerance (which, if you are like me, varies from minute to minute and from one market to another) and the particular assets you already happen to own.

There are five or six major stock sectors in the science-and-technology group, although they overlap and are loosely defined: software, biotech, computers and semiconductors, networking, and communications. Put about 15 percent of your portfolio into each technology group. Biotechs and computers tend to have opposite trading patterns, so when one group is down the other is likely to be up. With multiple groups (technological diversification), a portfolio remains fairly stable despite sharp excursions within specific sectors. If you are in cash for an extended period (for example, if you have taken profits in May and want to reserve some cash against the next winter's rally), park it in utility stocks or a utility fund. Over time, utilities tend to move opposite technologies, and provide excellent diversification for your portfolio in down periods for the science-and-technology group.

Such seat-of-the-pants methods of portfolio diversification are, incidentally, of the type called "naive" in texts. There is obviously an arched academic eyebrow implied by the choice of the term *naive*. True or "formal" portfolio diversification is a mathematically challenging technique that must take into account all of your assets. These include stocks, bonds, and insurance; illiquid assets such as real estate; plus variously invested IRAs, pensions, and whatever else you may have of value, such as a childhood stamp collection, a '57 Thunderbird roadster, or an attic full of antiques.

The mathematics of formal diversification is sensible and nicely conceived. But the "data in" tend to be a collection of really bad estimates. This is because any assessment of the volatility of so many different types of assets is likely to be inaccurate. So why bother?

It's worth a crack, because if you do not have some sort of logical handle on the mix of assets in your portfolio, you are probably risking too much money to achieve the returns you are getting. And if you are happy with the portfolio's risk level, consider the possibility that without taking on any additional risk, you could be enjoying better returns.

CDA Investment Technologies of Rockville, Maryland, a highly regarded investment service founded and staffed by mathematicians, publishes for financial planners a program called the Cadence Asset Mix Optimizer. This service costs many hundreds of dollars per year, and includes frequent data updates to reflect changes in the trading properties of various different kinds of assets. The price is obviously out of sight for an individual, who may need the information produced by the program a few times altogether.

Cadence is attractive to financial planners, however, because they encounter the diversification problem every day. Thus, your planner or your broker can run the Asset Mix Optimizer software for you, either on an IBM-PC compatible computer or, via modem link, on the CDA computers in Bethesda. So, formal diversification is probably not something you can do yourself, but you can have it done at quite reasonable cost without touching a computer. It is worth it because the result you get is unique to your own assets and goals.

Asset Mix Optimizer will review your existing (or hypothetical) asset mix and suggest adjustments you can make to improve it. The software can take into account the cost of selling one security to buy another. It uses performance data on thirty-two classes of assets: stocks in various sectors, mutual funds grouped by objective (growth, income, junk, global, and so on), metals, T-bills, municipal bonds, utilities, you name it.

It was from this program that I learned that my own portfolio, which is of course "overweighted" in science-and-technology stocks, could be balanced off for risk reduction by reallocating some of the assets into utility stocks. There is another point to be made here, which is the obvious one that not all of your money should be invested in science and technology. All of the money you earmark for "growth" should be. For most investors, this implies 15 percent to 20 percent of total equity assets.

The same methods of formal diversification used in the CDA Asset Mix Optimizer can be applied *in fine,* to the narrower problem of stock portfolio diversification. Again, why bother?

It is important to recognize that a portfolio of "good stocks" is not the same thing as a good stock portfolio. You could accumulate a portfolio of sixteen good oil stocks, for example, and watch in horror one day as the whole thing crashed on news from the Middle East. It is an obvious mistake to construct a specialized sector portfolio like this, but it is quite possible to make the same mistake by purchasing stocks that *look* different from one another, and are clearly in diverse businesses — yet move together as stocks in synchrony. Meaning, they topple together like bowling pins.

A good portfolio will contain a tightly calculated mix of paired stocks — stocks that tend to move in opposite directions in response to economic news. Pair an importer with an exporter, or, less obviously, a drug company with an electronics distributor. Easy as this may sound, you cannot do this kind of mixing and matching intuitively. Hence the need for a computer program.

Try The Sophisticated Investor, a PC program published by Miller Associates of Incline Village, Nevada. In about an hour in the public library, you can gather all the numbers it needs to be fed to make an evaluation of your stock portfolio.

The program evaluates the price history and weighting of your current stock portfolio and determines what the *ideal* weighting should be. Essentially, it asks if your existing portfolio is earning its keep. Does the portfolio generate a sufficient return to justify the risk you take, every day, by passively continuing to hold it? If not, the program will suggest ways to tune and prune it. The idea is to either produce a higher return at the same level of risk, or to produce the same return at a reduced level of risk. It is a great program to run if you happen to be in a selling mood, as it will spot and suggest the elimination of any marginal or redundant stocks. Such stocks either add nothing, or add nothing different to the portfolio.

PART TWO

THE MAJOR GROUPS

Chapter 8

Networks as Money Machines

EVERY SUCCESS STORY about a technology stock turns out to be, on closer examination, a story about a network. Computer networking stocks such as Cisco Systems, Novell, and Bay Networks are literal examples. IBM, in the heyday of its monopoly, created and maintained computer networks — not merely computers. Colossal technological monopolies in history, including the nineteenth-century railroads, the old AT&T telephone network, and the power companies, have all constituted networks. Television broadcasting companies and the cable systems that have supplanted them are all networks. Every company has some sort of sales and distribution network, and many complex, technology-based businesses (software, pharmaceuticals, intricate copying machines) are maintained by customer service and technical support networks.

The network concept is as old as the idea of a marketplace. Ancient cities, most notably ancient Rome, were configured in the form of a hub and spokes, with the marketplace at the center of the hub and a network of roads extending from that hub out into the empire. This hub-and-spokes network was an efficient machine that concentrated wealth at its center — that is, at the city center of Rome. The hub-and-spokes pattern is clearly recognizable in diagrammatic representations of individual computers, computer networks, airline networks, and railway networks. It is the trademark geometric shape of a monopoly.

Within a protected network, there is no price competition. To mentally test this idea, imagine yourself driving up to the row of toll-booths at the mouth of the Lincoln Tunnel. Do rival toll-takers compete here, crying out bids for your business? They do not. Are lots of lower-cost alternatives on offer? None. Pay the toll and drive into the tunnel.

The power to shut out price competition is inherent in the machinery of networks. They can charge whatever the traffic will bear. To prevent abuses of this power, many types of networks are regulated as common carriers by the government. Those networks that are unregulated are usually novel types of networks, and they tend to be excellent investments.

Roman roads, like the walls of China, were conceived and constructed as linear fortresses. They were trenched into the brows of hills in order to command high ground, and troops could be rapidly deployed to defend strategically important vantage points on every road. The Romans themselves did not call them Roman roads — they called them the Roman military highways. The defense of the network was crucial, for it was the pipeline system for the wealth of the nation. The expansion of the empire consisted of the expansion of the roadway network.

It was ultimately fifty thousand miles in extent. When the Romans lost control of it, the empire imploded. Long lines of Goths, Vandals, and other barbarians came pouring down the convenient, well-paved roads into Rome. In the late twentieth century much the same thing happened to IBM — and to its stock.

Modern commercial networks must, like the Roman roads, be defended to deny access to competitors (and freeloaders). AT&T fought tooth and nail in court to protect access to their proprietary phone network, which was one of the grandest monopolies in history. When divestiture was ordered, it had the intriguing effect of dissecting the great national network into seven smaller, inherently more efficient regional monopolies.

Railroad barons in nineteenth-century Britain sought to prevent access to their networks by means of engineering: they built their railways to a variety of incompatible gauges. In this century computer manufacturers and networkers have long attempted to secure their networks by similar means, that is, by deliberately engineering in incompatibility.

If access to a network cannot be gained or forced, sometimes that network can be bypassed by its competitors. When small computer manufacturers (Dell, Zeos, Gateway) found they had little hope of cracking into the Compaq-dominated network of retail computer dealerships, the insurgent manufacturers made use of commonplace preexisting networks to reach over the top of the retail dealer network — and gain direct access to customers. For shop windows, they used magazine advertisements. For a sales network, they used the telephone system. For a distribution network, they used the United States Mail and package delivery services such as UPS. And they won.

Technological competition is a complex board game that is all about creating networks and gaining access to, overgrowing, or bypassing existing networks and — above all — protecting access to proprietary networks. Here is an example that illustrates the economics of network building and the dollar value of protected access to a network.

After the divestiture of AT&T, many hundreds of small long-distance companies sprang into existence. As one might expect, consolidation ensued. We are down to about three hundred such companies now, and the business is still actively consolidating. For a tiny long-distance company with no extensive network of its own, the cost of network access might devour as much as 60 percent of gross revenues. It is no wonder that such a business may be only marginally profitable. But when one of these small companies is acquired by a larger one, its customer base suddenly can be made profitable — simply by plugging it into the larger, far more cost-efficient network of the acquiring company.

LDDS Communications of Jackson, Mississippi, put together in a vigorous acquisition program a new long-distance telephone network covering twenty-seven states. Each (struggling, marginal) acquired company became profitable the instant it gained access to the burgeoning LDDS network. It is as though LDDS had a Midas touch, but the newfound money arose from the combinatorial logic of their protected network. Join the network — stop disbursing 60 percent of revenues to the bigger guys. That simple. Not incidentally, LDDS's stock became an institutional darling. In four years of particularly vigorous growth, the stock climbed 2,627 percent. For a $1,000 investment, a $25,272 gain.

A profitable modern network is a triumph, and the technology on which it is based can dazzle the beholder into thinking that the wealth created by the network was actually, somehow, created by its technology: by its particular phalanx of wizards, its circuits, its software. To see through the technology to the underlying business principle, it is helpful to examine simpler networks that thrived long ago. I find the most readily understood network technologies, as businesses, were the railways, and the simplest of all was the first one.

Its image is preserved in an old print. The world's first commercial railway network was a circular exhibition track constructed in London in 1808 by locomotive inventor Richard Trevithick. A tiny locomotive, called the "Catch-me-who-can," pulled a few passenger carts around the circle. The track was surrounded by a tall fence. Trevithick sold tickets through a window in this fence to Londoners who paid a few pence just to get in and marvel at this self-propelled gadget puffing around its circuit at 12 mph.

The steam engine was a transforming technology, no question, but it is the *fence* that has endured as a feature of modern networks. By blocking the view, by thwarting free access, the fence transformed Trevithick's little railway network from a public spectacle into a profitable private business.

In proprietary computer networks, the fence takes the form of compatibility barriers. Any useful network can be made profitable so long as access can be controlled. Protected network access has been the governing principle of Roman roads, modern toll roads, telephone and cellular phone networks, broadcasting networks, marketing and distribution networks, oil and gas pipelines, and computer networks. As an investor, the nature and controllability of the network is the first thing you must consider in evaluating any technology stock.

Forget sales, earnings, and the price of the stock. Start by trying to identify and understand the underlying network. Only in the context of a network will the numbers make sense. The first question is always one of network access. Is it controlled? Can it be brought or kept under control? In short, is there a fence around the business?

There appears to be a deep-set problem with competing technological networks that mature simultaneously, as the railways did in the nineteenth century. They outgrow their own success. At a certain critical point, a network suddenly becomes too big for any single entrepreneur to control. The network is transformed by fusion into a common carrier, a shared public utility, and the private company or companies that originally created it lose the power to control access to their formerly captive customers.

As an investor, you can foresee this network overgrowth problem by glancing at a map or diagram. If it is a distinct hub-and-spokes pattern, fine. But notice that when you superimpose several proprietary hub-and-spokes networks, the multiple wagonwheel patterns get lost in a welter of crisscrossed lines. A widespread grid emerges — that is, a network without a center. This Cartesian grid is a danger signal for investors.

A superb example can be seen in a railway map of the United States in 1912, the zenith year for railway technology and railroad companies' success. These old maps are amazing. The rails went *everywhere*. One might call such a universal gridwork a supernet. No one company can monopolize a supernet, because wherever the lines of the grid intersect, access is breached and an alternative route is created. The customer has two ways to go — a choice.

Alternatives compete. Competition lowers prices for goods and services. Declining profits damage earnings. Damaged earnings sink stocks. The railroads peaked as a business in 1912. This was eight years before the country had roads good enough to bear trucks, let alone truck traffic, from city to city. Competition arose within the railway network because multiple networks had become so extensive, they had overgrown each other. Then, when the roadway network was superimposed on the railway network in the 1920s, the competition became devastating and recovery became impossible.

The sudden proliferation of microcomputers — almost two hundred million of them — is actively forcing the interconnection of computers and networks into supernets: networks too large and diffuse to be controlled by any single company. The process has acquired the restless energy of a social force. Among other things, it is rapidly breaking down technical and commercial barriers against the interconnection of different manufacturers' computers and networks.

Interconnection instantly reduces the power of invested capital to profit in captive markets. But it simultaneously enhances potential returns on capital by opening up access to competitors' markets. When a supernet emerges, the investor should move money away from the established monopoly stocks and into the stocks of monopoly breakers.

Supernets emerge in two steps. Again, a helpful early example is the development of the railway networks in the nineteenth century.

First, many proprietary railroad networks sprouted simultaneously from major metropolitan hubs. Then, when these proprietary networks grew large enough to crowd each other and to intersect, they suddenly fused to form supernets — nationwide railway networks. We are now approaching this same critical passage in the growth of computer networks.

Thoughtful, visionary John Sculley, during his tenure as the head of Apple Computer, described to me the formation of the supernets as a crucial, nation-building technology: "The railway. The industry is going ahead right now. The cables are being laid. Standards are being set. Much of the hardware is built, much of the software is already written.

"What the supernets will do for the country, in knitting together industry and finance and the schools — in accelerating the economy — is so absolutely and emphatically important that it is almost beyond our present understanding."

But what about incompatibility? The history of the railway networks offers an insight. The largest incompatible railway network in nineteenth-century England was the Great Western Railway, or GWR. It was constructed by the brilliant engineer Isambard Kingdom Brunel, beginning in 1835. He set his rails seven feet apart, and began running huge locomotives up and down these wide tracks in 1838. It was his intention, in selecting the broad gauge, to protect his network and his markets from competitive access. Of course Brunel never said this. He said bigger trains were better trains.

After Brunel built the GWR, almost all subsequent construction by other railways in Great Britain was standardized at a narrower gauge of 4 feet, 8½ inches, and this ultimately became the "standard" gauge for the nation's railway network.

Brunel continued to argue that he had developed a superior railway technology. He was quite right, incidentally. His broader-gauge tracks accommodated bigger engines and, because of the sheer colossal breadth of their fireboxes, they pulled harder and ran faster than contemporary narrow-gauge locomotives. Fully two decades before the American Civil War, Brunel's strange locomotives (they looked like gigantic medieval cannons) were routinely transporting goods and passengers in and out of London at average speeds near 60 mph.

Yet, ultimately, the performance of these individual machines didn't count. What mattered more, then as now, was the performance of the network as a whole. The growth of the English railway network was confounded by the very existence of Brunel's incompatible broad-gauge tracks.

Brunel and his successors in the Great Western Railway put up a long and tenacious struggle, but on May 21, 1892, under the coercion of a parliamentary decree, the British railways were standardized to the narrow gauge. At Swindon, the terminus of the Great Western, special tracks were laid down to provide a parking place for fifteen solid miles of empty carriages and cold locomotives. It must have seemed the end of greatness for the Great Western Railway. But it wasn't. After a half-century of resisting it, the company converted its track gauge in one weekend. It quickly modified its cars and its engines and resumed operations.

So what had been demonstrated? Simply that network compatibility was more valuable to the market at large — the English nation in this case — than the isolated performance of any particular train-building technology, however wonderful.

The lesson for modern builders of computers and computer communication networks is not simply that engineered incompatibility ultimately fails as a device to protect access to the network. This truism should surprise no one. What's interesting about the end of the Great Western's broad gauge is not the fact but the *timing* of its demise. So long as the Great Western was a proprietary hub-and-spokes network, no real problems arose over the incompatibility of its broad gauge. But when other railway networks, expanding from urban hubs both north and south of the GWR, began to intersect at various points with the Great Western's private wagon wheel, real trouble started.

The inconvenience of the "break in gauge" at Gloucester, for example, where the Great Western track first intersected with standard-gauge lines from the Midlands and the north of England, turned the gauge issue into a noisy public cause. At Gloucester, all passengers had to change trains, and all freight had to be transshipped. The outcry from the customers was the nineteenth-century equivalent of today's vocal complaints from computer users that their machines won't readily "talk to each other."

The intersection problems grew worse as the GWR sprouted lines northward toward areas of industry, through Oxford and Birmingham, until finally intersections of broad- and narrow-gauge tracks were impending over a wide area of the south Midlands. It was at this point that Parliament finally had to force the GWR into conformity with the rest of the network.

The change in gauge particularly affected the GWR, but the real and underlying change was deeper, broader — and structural. The GWR was attempting to resist a global transition in the very nature of the English railway network. The change was taking place all over the system, not just in GWR territory, and it resulted directly from the increasing number of intersections of proprietary networks. It was a change in identity. A collection of formerly isolated wagon-wheel networks was suddenly fusing into a pervasive nationwide gridwork: a supernet.

In the United States, the problem of incompatible railway gauges was solved at one stroke by the government's selection of a standard gauge for the transcontinental railway. At the time (1862), fully 50 percent of U.S. railways were out of conformity with the government's choice of a standard transcontinental gauge. But within two decades, the U.S. railway network was unified by the universally accepted gauge standardized by the transcontinental line.

Some computer industry observers see this as a model for the standardization and, ultimately, unification of U.S. computer and communication networks into a sort of grand national brain. The government is one of the largest customers for information services, and technical and security standards already defined for government purchases could become pervasive. This is one possible avenue to technological compatibility: government-decreed adherence to some common standard "gauge" for computer communications. Industry also strives toward common compatibility standards — but it doesn't really want them. Why should it, when standardization brings an automatic decline in profitability? Industry groups regularly coalesce, splinter, and reform in alliances nominally directed to the goal of universal "open system" compatibility standards. It is not surprising that these coalitions of competitors somehow never quite settle on that common set of compatibility standards. It doesn't matter. Technology is about to blow past the politics of compatibility. As microprocessors grow more powerful — so powerful they can mimic each other — today's issues of compatibility will simply vanish.

As a basis for predicting what will happen next in the computer networking business, it is tempting to directly overlay the nineteenth-century experience on that of today, and to trace the consequences of sudden universal compatibility.

But the railway metaphor must not be taken perfectly literally. The emergence of an information supernet will be peculiar to our own times and technologies. The same forces are certainly at work: vigorous growth; troublesome intersections of competing networks; an opening up of competitive access to markets formerly held captive; and an urgently felt common effort — even a national priority — to knit together a new kind of economy. Unlike railways, however, computer manufacturers do not directly derive significant revenues from the continuing operation of the existing computer systems — only from their maintenance, support, and expansion into new or larger applications.

For the bigger computer manufacturers, networking was a truly attractive concept only when it was accomplished by linking computers of their own proprietary manufacture. Links to competitive computers chiefly have the effect of bringing competitors' computers — and pricing — into the center of their customers' fields of view. To the customer it means convenient communication between his own computers, and competitively priced data management. To the established manufacturer it just means trouble: technical problems and price competition. To an investor in any formerly proprietary network, compatibility means the network service or product has been opened up to price competition, and the time has come to sell the stock.

Yet at this late date, the creation and manufacture of incompatible computer products amounts to climbing out on a limb and sawing oneself off. Incompatibility is a tradition. It is not some dimly understood, decidedly hostile force of nature. It is a quality that is carefully engineered by human beings in the hope of protecting their markets. There is nothing wrong with this. Up to a certain point, it works. But beyond that point the forces of the market favor the formation of supernets.

The lessons for investors seem clear. A specific network-using device always matters less than the profitability of the network it plies. Trucks, trains, jets, television transmitters, phones, and computers are all very interesting as machines, but they do not constitute the machinery of the economy. The machines that concentrate money are roads, rails, airways, channels, phone lines, and computer links — the networks. Kept distinct, they are kept profitable. When they are overlaid they must compete, and profitability declines.

Proprietary networks and high profitability are linked absolutely. A company's proprietary network, profits, and stock all fall down when access to the network can no longer be protected. This may happen when the network is opened up (as, for example, to compatible computers), when it is bypassed by another network, or when it simply grows large enough to interpenetrate other hub-and-spokes networks.

In an airline network, for example, the hub-and-spokes system stops being profitable when upstart competitors begin flying in obnoxious little hops from spoke to spoke. Southwest Airlines is famous for this, and famously profitable in a dismally unprofitable industry. Southwest is a network breaker, and about as popular among other airlines as a pirate ship. Finally, competition between private and public networks is devastating to the private networks. The railroads were devastated, as businesses, by the public highway system.

The hottest technology stocks are always those in companies that have successfully created and then protected networks — or have figured out a way to defeat a network-based monopoly by opening access to the markets that some network has held captive.

With regard to stocks in computer companies and networks, I would avoid placing bets on any side of the compatibility wars. We have entered a period in computer technology, perhaps analogous to the early 1900s in the railroad business, when monopolies and even profitable pricing are becoming more and more difficult to sustain. Apple, Intel, Motorola, IBM, and Digital all offer their own standard of hardware compatibility, and various software companies, including Microsoft and Novell, are urging their own rival systems for uniting these many systems into some universally acceptable whole.

The outcome, which is compatibility, is a foregone conclusion. Favor the stocks of those companies — and they are not necessarily computer or networking companies — who recognize at the strategic level that the intersection of data and communications networks simultaneously creates a broad new market and a wholly new product. And that this product, which is a supernet, is coming into the world like an avalanche.

Chapter 9

The Computer Networks

STOCKS IN MODERN COMPUTER "networking" companies do not derive their commercial energy and profits from creating networks. It should be understood that they are completing the destruction of networks — old-fashioned restricted-access networks put into place in past decades by established mainframe and mini-computer manufacturers such as IBM and Digital Equipment.

Access to such networks was restricted in the sense that once you installed an IBM system in your corporation, you were committed to adding only IBM or strictly IBM-compatible equipment as your internal network expanded.

Customers may have resented their captivity, but there was little to be done about it as long as the computer manufacturers were able to maintain the engineered-in incompatibility of their respective systems. What does "compatibility" really mean? Two compatible computers will communicate and work together. But put yourself behind the eyes of a minicomputer or mainframe manufacturer. If your competitor's machine can "understand" and communicate with your machine, then that understanding, communicating rival machine can also *replace* your machine. Price competition may be expected to ensue. Your monopoly, and the benefits to you of monopoly pricing, are both lost. Hence, the idea of two computers that freely "talk to each other" was abhorrent to big computer makers.

When a network cannot be cracked, it can be overgrown and supplanted. In the railroad wars of the last century, for example, it was not uncommon for one railroad to construct a line precisely paralleling that of a competitor. This was done as a means to force access into a market — a city — formerly captive to the original railway line and network.

The mainframe and minicomputer networks of the mid-twentieth century are being overgrown and supplanted by networks of desktop computers. Small networks typically unite twelve or thirteen desktop computers, and there are at this writing about 1.5 million such networks. They have already displaced the minicomputer networks — and have virtually foreclosed on minicomputer manufacturing as a viable business.

Small networks are connected through a device called an intelligent hub. These hubs are simply points of convergence, with multiple sockets for cables linking the desktop computers. The market for these hubs is estimated to be worth $350 million annually. SynOptics Communications of Santa Clara, California, essentially defined the intelligent-hub business, and captured the lion's share of the early market for hubs. (It merged with Wellfleet Communications in 1994 to form Bay Networks.) Before SynOptics, computers were commonly linked into local area networks in the manner of series-connected strings of Christmas tree lights. You remember them: if one goes out, they all go out. The SynOptics approach (which ultimately came to be recognized as a new standard in networks of this type, called the 10BASE-T standard) used ordinary telephone cable to link the machines to a central hub. The hub was provided with sufficient electronic intelligence to enable the network to maneuver around the inevitable breakdowns on individual spokes.

For midrange systems, the hub-and-spoke technology provides a way to link the computers with ordinary phone wires rather than elaborate custom cable installations. SynOptics concentrated on quality products, kept prices at a premium, and prospered. So did the stock. But then came Cabletron Systems, a scrappy and enterprising New Hampshire company. Through hard selling and aggressive pricing, Cabletron quickly claimed a great big piece of the pie — and the pie has segmented, now, among at least thirty different other makers of intelligent hubs. In other words, the intelligent-hub bonanza turned into a melee, a perfectly typical pattern for technology businesses.

Yet there is a second component to the networking business that has progressed with serene dignity and enormous profitability. This is the business of providing network routers, as practiced by relatively few companies, including Cisco Systems.

Internetworking routers can be understood as simultaneous translators for network languages, rather like the human simultaneous interpreters at the United Nations. They enable a company to link diverse local networks into a single unified network including, for example, the Macintoshes of the marketing department, the IBM or DEC systems in finance, and the Sun workstations in engineering. It is precisely this service — this power to force computers of diverse manufacture to communicate — that has provided the cash propulsion for computer networking. There are two good ways to make a fortune: by making a monopoly and by smashing a monopoly. The router is a manufactured device that is programmed to break up monopolies. The companies that make routers — especially Cisco — are high among the most successful stock market gainers of the late twentieth century.

What protects the router business is its enormous difficulty — not patents, copyrights, or proprietary hardware. Software that is very hard to write is very hard to match, especially when the writers have a long head start, as Cisco's pioneering programmers certainly do. But will these networking businesses continue to be top producing stocks as we move into the next century? Probably not.

It was the collapse of the older networks — the hissing escape of captive customers under pressure — that originally energized the success of Cisco, SynOptics, Cabletron, and their brethren. It is a situation analogous to the growth of the public highway network in the United States. It overgrew and supplanted the nineteenth-century railway networks, and it thereby destroyed what little was left of the railway monopolies. Contractors made money building the roads. But once the public roads were in place, no new monopoly arose from them. Access to the new roadway network was unlimited. So, too, with the polyglot computer networks that are emerging today. Where there is no limit to access to a network, the network has no power to monopolize the market it serves. In other words, the networking stocks are a play on a remarkable late-twentieth-century trend. They are fine to own, for a while, but they are not buy-and-hold stocks for your children's portfolios.

The popular notion of "interoperable" networked computers can be reinterpreted by individual manufacturers (given a normal healthy level of marketing paranoia) as a trend toward interchangeable computers. This is why the more established manufacturers have tended to recoil from it or even, perhaps, to deny to themselves or to some of their own people that it is really happening.

Open interconnection and open competition is very much in the interest of smaller, newer companies selling smaller, newer computers. It is no accident that the supernet concept finds its most vigorous proponents among desktop computer manufacturers; it is a wedge into markets formerly isolated by technical incompatibility with their products.

John Sculley remarked to me: "There isn't any company in the world that is more impacted by this than IBM."

Because it is the largest manufacturer of large computers, IBM has the most at stake. IBM's senior mainframe and minicomputer markets are the most widely infiltrated from below — and these had been IBM's most profitable lines. The company is nevertheless actively urging industry network and communication standards, and it is IBM that gave the microcomputer revolution its strongest impetus. The company appears to be in conflict with itself on this issue, but its overall self-interest would seem to call for a delaying action in the trend to supernets.

A similar conflict affected Digital Equipment. "DEC is in a funny situation here," Hambrecht & Quist computer analyst Robert Herrick explained to me at the beginning of the decade. "At the high end of the market, where they compete with IBM, interoperability works to their advantage in opening up new business. But at the low end, in workstations, interoperability is a defensive posture. They are opening themselves up to competition, from Sun Micro Systems for example, by offering compatible workstations."

Then what happened? When it became clear to the stock market that DEC was indeed opening up IBM's market to its own Digital Equipment products, it seemed to have an impact like unto that of Admiral Perry opening up Japan. Digital's stock started climbing from a 1984 low of $31, at the bottom of a pervasive slump in technology stocks. It kept climbing — soaring, finally, in just four years, to an amazing pinnacle near $200. Evidently the investors, eyeing IBM's profit margins, jumped to the conclusion that if Digital could now compete at last for the same customers, DEC would enjoy margins just like IBM's.

Not surprisingly, it did not turn out that way. When a monopoly breaks, it pops like a balloon. The stocks of both IBM and Digital have essentially declined ever since. If the twilight of the great railroads occurred in 1912, then perhaps the twilight of the "big iron" computer business came in 1990. IBM and Digital are very different companies today, and they have both learned to sell small compatible computers as commodity products.

While these two titans circled and then engaged each other, the real issue of the future of the computer business seems to have been resolved at approximately the level of their ankles, among the tiny and, in those days, not-to-be-taken-very-seriously microcomputer sellers and their customers. (IBM was itself one such microcomputer seller — a pioneer — and it can be argued that the company suffered because it did not take its own PC seriously enough.)

Already in 1990, microcomputers were everywhere, but microcomputer power was going to waste in isolation. Work cranked out on a microcomputer stopped there. Results had to be laboriously extracted from the machine before they could be passed to other computers. And much data that might be processed on the microcomputer could not find an easy way to get *into* the microcomputer. The desktops destroyed the old computer monopolies, which were based on hub-and-spokes networks within corporations. But in the course of destroying the monopolies, the desktops also destroyed, by utter fragmentation, the useful communication technology the networks had always provided.

In businesses of all sizes, microcomputers became magnets for interconnecting wires. They begged to be networked. Just now the business community is saturated with microcomputers, and the demand for networks to pull them together is not merely strong: it has produced the best technology business, the fastest growth, and the hottest technology stocks of this decade. Each desktop microcomputer is potentially a node in a network; and a vigorous subindustry, led by Novell and Cisco Systems, has grown around the practice of linking micros into local and wide-area networks. Right now, the creation of compatibility is a hugely successful industry in its own right.

This is what Cisco, Bay Networks, and several other networking companies do for a living. With translation software, they enable computers of many different kinds to talk to each other. Cisco Systems is perhaps the prototype networking stock of the current era. It was issued in early 1990 at a split-adjusted $2.75. It essentially ascended in a straight line from this value, and four years later it was trading near $75. For a $1,000 investment, a $25,180 return.

The blossoming local area nets of PCs made a strong bid for new applications business — computer sales that might have, until the late 1980s, gone straight to the minicomputer and mainframe manufacturers. According to Rod Canion (then chairman of Compaq, now a consultant to the computer industry), the emergence of networked desktops challenged the mainframe and especially the minicomputer manufacturers because "It opens up their captive area. As new applications come along, nets and PCs will be preferred. It's probably the most powerful force at work in the computer industry: this undeniable upward march of PC power, especially when the PCs are networked together."

It would be conceivable for microcomputer networks to simply overgrow and supplant the existing, senior lines of mainframe and minicomputer networks. They have already extinguished much of the minicomputer business. Mainframes hold out because they are uniquely able to handle so-called mission-critical applications such as airline reservation and credit-card billing systems. But no one can say this business, too, will not one day migrate to nets of powerful microcomputers.

Special, extremely powerful microcomputers, often equipped with multiple microprocessors, are styled as "superservers." They are now being manufactured by many competing firms, and they represent the last step in the transition from the older, proprietary minicomputer networks to pervasively linked networks of microcomputers. These powerful, supremely reliable microcomputers can link networks of up to three hundred users. (A typical local area network has only about ten users.)

The difference between a superserver and a minicomputer, in terms of computing power, is not great. Both are big, potent machines. The distinction is rather one of generations and of technical politics. Superservers belong to the culture and technology of networked microcomputers. Minicomputers belong to the older culture of proprietary networks that are being pushed aside.

Manufacturers of superservers include Compaq (currently the dominant player), Netframe Systems, and Tricord. The field is eventually going to be a crowded one, but it is still quite profitable in the mid-1990s; these companies are attractive as investments. Compaq simply already owns the largest share of this market. It sells $1.2 billion worth of servers annually.

Tricord has annual sales of $90 million — less business, but better growth potential. It has excellent superserver technology, multiple customers, and an open growth path. However, it is a relatively new issue and a volatile stock.

IBM seems ambivalent about developing a business in superservers, perhaps because they compete with its senior lines of big machines. But they are in it. It is a lesson of history. England's broadgauge Great Western Railway would probably have been bypassed and cut off by narrow-gauge operators, had the Great Western not at the last moment capitulated to parliamentary pressure and adjusted their gauge to make it compatible with that of intersecting networks' tracks. Most manufacturers would rather settle for half a loaf — or a third, or a fourth, or the nth part of however monstrous a supernet finally does emerge.

For this is the logical direction networking takes. When the lines "go everywhere," as the railways once did, we will have completed a supernet. When it happens, people will come to regard the minicomputer and mainframe computer businesses in the same, sadly bemused way they now regard the American railroads — as relics of an ancient, lost, romantic age of robber barons, great steam-belching machines the size of dinosaurs, huge profits, and dazzling stock plays.

Having foreseen this nostalgia, it is important to recognize that it is not really appropriate as yet, nor are things quite that simple. The minicomputer business is indeed doomed, but the mainframe business is still viable. It is contracting, but the contraction itself, as with any other major change, has created a business opportunity. At this point, it is estimated that 80 percent of all corporate data still resides on storage devices attached to mainframe computers — yet mainframes cannot readily communicate over distances greater than four hundred feet. To communicate across the country, they require devices called channel extenders. Computer Network Technology of Maple Grove, Minnesota, makes channel extenders to link one mainframe to another; or a mainframe to a remote supercomputer; or a mainframe to a remote network of desktops.

Why is this a growth technology? Because the mainframe computer is not quite dead after all. In fact, the idea that the mainframe is a goner has long been a stock market cliché, and it is often very wise to bet against long-standing generalizations about stock market sectors.

Recall the remarkable growth in the 1980s of on-line processing for automatic teller machine transactions and for airline reservation systems. Note that BankAmerica, as a single example, must process twenty million debits and credits to its checking and savings accounts each day. Such high-volume processing is obviously a mainframe computing problem — and it often requires long-distance communication lines.

The trend to on-line processing happened to coincide with the merger boom of the 1980s, which made many corporate mainframe computer centers redundant. To cut costs, many corporations have since been consolidating their mainframe computer centers and moving them to outlying areas.

When a mainframe is deleted from a data-gathering system, its tasks are usually assumed by another, remote mainframe. When this happens, business information has to travel a long way. Mainframe computers are indeed shrinking in number, but with each incremental contraction of the mainframe population, the market for high-speed communication grows.

Computer Network Technology's customers are concentrated in energy, telecommunications, and financial services. For a small company, its customer list reads like a corporate *Who's Who:* Shell Oil, Morgan Stanley, Pacific Bell, Cray Research, Mitsubishi, MCI, U.S. Sprint, and AT&T. A typical single sale is worth $350,000, and orders of $1 million or more are not unusual. Over half of all equipment sales in a year represent repeat business. The most common installation extends an IBM mainframe channel over unlimited distances using high-speed common carrier links such as leased high-capacity phone lines.

Computer Network's chief executive, McKenzie Lewis, is an IBM alumnus. Because his firm's revenue arrives in such big chunks, the quarter-to-quarter performance is volatile — meaning unpredictable. Sometimes, it seems Wall Street values predictability over profitability — and the Street also loves succinct broadsides such as "mainframes are over." Perhaps for these reasons, the stock was widely underrated. We were able to double our money on it in the course of one year.

Right now, computer networks are in real disarray. The tidy but archaic image of multiple proprietary wagon-wheel networks, each self-contained and private, has given way to a new picture — networks networked to networks. This is both as wonderful and as messy as it sounds. The very idea of the standalone computer as a unique entity has begun to fade. In the end, your own computer will simply provide access to computing power available "out there on the network." An Apple will get you a piggyback ride on a Cray.

The trouble is, the proprietary values set afloat in the netherworld of the network — such as proprietary computer programs and financial assets in the process of being transferred electronically — may get lost or stolen. The vast interconnection of computer systems greatly multiplies our ability to compute, process, and transfer information. But it also vastly multiplies our vulnerability to breaches of privacy and outright piracy.

There are two answers to the network security problem: tremendous expansion of distinct corporate communication nets, or a massive and successful encoding of all proprietary information. Coding costs less. Stock pickers eyeing the information highway, the emergence of various wired and wireless information access systems, and the future of networking generally should consider this issue of security as a gate question.

Networks are profitable only when they are secured against competitive access. But interestingly, the security the networks can be made to provide inherently is becoming an important part of their service and their commercial appeal. Marginally profitable services can be restored to profitability by offering them as secured products on a network. This possibility is extremely significant just now to the software industry, where it is believed that as many as half the programs in use are illicit copies. Programs offered as network services, rather than products, are far less likely to become mass-marketed freebies.

Ultimately, when computer and communication networks can be made as secure as, say, the U.S. Mail, networks will break out beyond their present corporate boundaries and fuse into a practical, pervasive societywide supernet. Internal corporate networks will be tied into the major communication networks, i.e., the telecommunication and cable systems. The most dramatic growth statistics may then shift from what we think of as "the networking stocks" (Cisco, Novell, Bay Networks) to global networks reaching far beyond the corporate peripheries: specifically, that is, to the telecommunication and cable networks.

Chapter 10

The Picture Machines

IN A GRAND SWIRL OF PLANS and hypes and touts and techno-cheerleading, the Information Century is fast coming upon us. The difficulty is, the concept hasn't quite gelled, and tidal surges of money are washing back and forth across the television and telecommunications stock scene. Investors and institutions are naturally foraging for opportunities, for fresh starts, and for the large share of market that will automatically accrue to whichever corporation or coalition figures this thing out first. So here is an important passage in our society, but it reads rather like an important passage from *Alice in Wonderland*.

We shall be wired. No, we shall be wireless. Or no again, we shall be cabled together, or yet again, wired and cabled and wireless all at once. There shall be a library metaphor instead of a broadcast metaphor. We are observing the emergence and convergence of information nets and supernets, highways and superhighways. But wait — make sure to register the subtle but not-to-be ignored global paradigm shift. And so on.

There is a lot of hype in this field, whatever it is, and a lot of large thinking, and (inevitably) a lot of stock scamming. It will get worse. But it isn't just hype. Every investor can see there is something important going on. The question is, precisely where in this information cosmos are we supposed to invest our hard-won earthly money?

We have some basic guidelines from history, from investment experience, and from common business sense. For example, we know it is networks, not devices, that make money over time. We also know that the commercial value of a network, and its rate of return to stockholders, depends on secured access above all else. Restricted access is most readily assured with closed pipes such as telephone lines and fiber-optic cables, or by wireless broadcasting of information that has been very well encrypted.

What is the common quality of the information to be shipped over these lines, cables, or encrypted wireless channels? It is largely pictorial. The terms for the new technologies are, variously, *interactive TV, cable PC, graphical user interfaces, high-definition television,* and so on in this vein. So we need to be thinking about pictures.

Two things about pictures are not immediately obvious. First, a picture is much more expensive to transmit than a verbal message. It is expensive both in a literal sense and in terms of the technical resources it takes to do the job. This is because pictures are heavy with data. They are made up of millions of bits of information. The volume of data in a stream of pictures (e.g., a television show) is incredible, and calls for a broadband transmission medium, such as (almost ideally) a fiber-optic cable. In trade slang, a broad-bandwidth transmission medium is a "fat pipe."

Pictures are less easily transmitted by wire or by wireless at television broadcast frequencies, and so when a picture stream is transmitted via these relatively narrow-bandwidth media, it is usually cut down, abbreviated, or abridged in some way. Only a fraction of the visual information impinging on the TV camera makes it through the transmission medium to the viewer watching a TV screen. This is why any 35mm slide looks so much better than the picture on your TV set.

People crave richer pictures. In a casual conversation, a CompuServe marketing executive remarked to me that the company was often surprised to see which products and services succeeded best on their hugely diverse and popular compendium of on-line services. CompuServe's revenue stream is a function of access time — the amount of time computer users spend gazing at or downloading CompuServe's material on-line — so the company naturally pays attention to what works.

Through CompuServe, for example, an investor might choose to view stock quotes, the balance sheets or relative performance of public companies, or current business news-wire stories. Users with other interests, from airline schedules to stamps to weather to putting up peaches, can dial CompuServe for information of particular interest to them. The active subscription base is probably in the high hundreds of thousands of computerists.

The big recent surprise, my friend said, was the sudden and overwhelming success of on-line libraries of images — pictures and photographs. Computers of the current generation can put images on their screens of extremely high quality. Such images are barely distinguishable from a 35mm slide projection — crystal clear, crisply defined, and colorful.

CompuServe users quickly discovered they had a great appetite for such images, and they were, and are, spending a great deal of time on-line downloading them to their screens and disks. My friend was shaking his head at the success of this new product — he said he would never have guessed it would happen. Given television's power to pump out pictures at the rate of 60 frames per second or 3,600 frames per minute, practically for free, why would CompuServe subscribers take the time (and pay for the time) to treasure a still?

This is not an idle question. It carries some clues for investors about the future course of computer and media technology.

The still novel practice of downloading high-quality, crystal-clear visual images has been little publicized, except in the odd, occasional, and invariably hand-wringing newspaper piece deploring the emergence, from the back streets onto the information highway, of on-line pornography. This is a moral point that needs to be made, but it somewhat obscures the main point, which is that human beings have a huge appetite for pictures, and not just dirty pictures.

We are, ourselves, inside our heads, image-processing machines. The compelling urge to make and to examine pictures has driven countless commercial success stories: photography, magazines, television, copying machines, coffee table books, and so on ad infinitum. The associated stock stories are legend: Kodak, Polaroid, Xerox, CBS, and RCA for starters. Two hundred years ago, there were just two sources for imagery: mirrors and art. Now we are surrounded and bombarded by multiple images from many different media. Yet it seems the visual appetite is never satisfied.

The computer, as a medium, has evolved rapidly over the past decade from a text-based device into a graphics-based device. Put another way, computers used to be language machines — now they are picture machines. The process began when Apple and, much later, Microsoft adopted the concept of a graphical user interface. (The idea was originally conceived by researchers at Xerox's Palo Alto Research Center.)

Improved computer graphics puts images on the PC screen that are a lot more literal — more true to life — than they were at the outset of personal computing. Take word processing. It used to be that the text on the computer screen had the unique and typical appearance of computer-generated text — bright, illuminated phosphors formed the impression of individual characters reversed out of a dark background field. But with today's word-processing programs, the screen image looks like a piece of white paper with inked characters impressed upon its surface.

Literal, high-resolution, photographic-quality images contain millions more bits of information than images consisting only of text characters. They also bear more information than the fuzzy, dodgy images received on television sets. It takes a comparatively long time — several seconds — to paint a computer screen with a high-resolution image resembling a 35mm slide. It is so very much slower than a television set because it presents so much more information. Apparently, this is what the brain is really hungry for. More detail.

The image on the TV screen is painted very rapidly, but viewers want it to change almost before it is completed. Lightning-quick cuts, dazzling zooms in and out, lap dissolves — all these video editing and framing tricks create the impression that things are changing even as you watch, that something new is coming. But that new thing never arrives, or at least, never comes fast enough. Viewers sit with a leaden thumb on the channel changer, flipping images constantly, looking for novelty. Children raised on television may let the channel changer rest on MTV, where image shifts are inherently so frenetic that mature adults must turn aside. MTV is a fad festival, a nonstop celebration of flux.

So how does it happen that a still photograph, patiently downloaded from CompuServe or some other on-line computer service, and paid for, can successfully compete for anyone's attention with the 3,600 half-formed images that television flashes for free in a single minute? Is it possible that a single clear, *National Geographic*–quality photographic image is what the channel changers are actually hunting for? Probably.

The content of a postcard landscape may be ridiculed as cornball subject matter, but it is a four-course dinner for the eye. It contains millions of bits of information. Compared to a photograph, TV is an endless conveyor of visual snacks. The key problem is the rate of delivery. Television delivers very little information in one second, a succession of rough sketches. The brain of a jaded viewer cannot bear to sit still waiting for the image to be completed. The image is never completed — the medium is incapable of carrying sufficient information to finish the job in the allotted time. And so the brain, looking for something more, tells the thumb to hit the channel flipper. It may be that the extraordinary success of cartoons on television has something to do with their diagrammatic quality. As information, they are much simpler than literal images, and so they can be completely conveyed by the limited, narrowband medium provided by broadcast television.

In contrast to a television picture, a sharp photograph delivers so much information that it cannot be absorbed in one second. People may sit and pore over it, sometimes for whole minutes, picking up the minutest details. They keep photographs in albums and return to them again and again. The subject of the pictures matters, but the amount of information it contains matters more.

The technology of manipulating and presenting high-resolution screen images has been well pioneered in the professions that need it: examples include medical imaging, photo processing for publication, military surveillance and targeting, computer-aided engineering, geology, and movie making. It now seems just a matter of time before high-resolution television finally arrives in some form as a popular medium. The actual device that delivers these images will be somewhat like a computer and somewhat like a TV set.

But it doesn't really matter what the device is — the business that will profit from this technology over time is the network that transports the pictures. It is the familiar network investment concept. Ignore the train. Buy the tracks.

The great question at this point is, what are the tracks going to look like? Because of the sheer volume of information that must be shipped, the network must be configured more like an electronic pipeline than an ordinary phone line. What works?

Part of the solution is broadband fiber-optic cable, some of which is already in place in networks operated by cable TV companies. The shift from wire to fiber optics means a change in rate of bit delivery from tens of kilobits per second to *gigabits* per second.

There are also technically clever approaches involving extremely-high-frequency wireless broadcasting and rebroadcasting. They seem to make sense as technologies, but from a business standpoint they are less promising. The problem is not just to deliver detailed images at high speed. The problem is to deliver them at a profit. This means access must be restricted, as it must be in every commercial network. The easiest and most direct way to secure a network is by means of closed pipes or cables. Information broadcast through the air is always at risk from interception, electrical noise, and competition from any wired services that happen to go to the same places.

In the past, wireless networks have competed most successfully with wired networks only in situations where the receiver moves about or is fixed in some extremely remote area, like the Australian outback. Radio broadcasting has survived as a business, in one view, because of the huge audience that enjoys listening to car radios and portables. The same story has been retold in the cellular phone business. Mobility is a trump card for wireless media, but where mobility does not matter — in fixed metropolitan installations — glass or copper wires make more sense.

Whichever medium turns out to be best, no single *existing* network is up to the task of maintaining a communication network in which high-resolution pictures are broadcast at the speed of full-motion video — let alone exchanged interactively. New networks must be built. The technologies appear to exist in pieces, however, and much of the capital investments in this field via the stock market has been placed with the idea of pulling together the right combination of technologies to make it all happen.

Phone companies have hub-and-spokes networks supported by highly evolved computerized switching technologies that enable messages to be routed from any incoming spoke to any outgoing spoke. But these are verbal messages or data feeds that can be easily fed down skimpy, narrow-bandwidth lines. To make the phone networks work for video signals, new broadband lines must be put in place.

The cable companies have some broadband lines already in place, but their networks resemble trees. Some of their lines branch from branches, rather than connect directly to the central trunk. These networks could deliver the pictures without difficulty, but they still lack the switching technology to produce interactivity. Hence the several proposed (and highly publicized) alliances between cable companies and phone companies. The idea is to combine cable's broadband transmission capability with telephone switching technology.

The commercial difference between telephone and cable TV systems is in the way they have chosen to protect access to their respective nets. Phone nets are protected because all message traffic must pass through the center — the hub — of a classical hub-and-spokes setup. The central hub is invisible to the phone users, but their calls are of course billed as they pass through the hub.

TV networks have no "traffic." They were conceived as broadcast media and they are protected at the periphery, rather than at the center. The familiar set-top box is the access port to the cable network, and it is also the toll gate.

Either type of commercial network could be adapted or perfected to carry interactive video or cable PC services. The telephone networks would have to replace their wire with "fat pipes." The cable companies would probably, in the end, find it helpful to reconfigure their networks into a classical hub-and-spokes pattern. It is not necessary to rewire a system to accomplish this change — technology exists to create a "virtual" hub-and-spokes system.

These stocks are volatile, but not really because the fusion of cable TV and telephone networks is such a great idea. The stocks swing because this new technology is being synthesized, by coalition and by acquisition, rather than invention. Buyouts and rumors of buyouts always make stocks go up, and frustrated buyouts always drop them back. The sheer scale of the capital involved certainly gets the attention of the stock market.

Meantime, the extent of the commerce in pictures that will traverse the new networks is not clearly defined. Movies on demand, interactive gambling and gaming, various library services, education, and retailing have all been advanced as attractive concepts for mass markets.

But the power to send and receive pictorial information is also being advanced from a different point of view, which is that of business computerists. In this view of the future, the material to be distributed over the information networks is not the prepackaged product of educators, entertainers, and the gaming industries; rather, it is the constant, daily, point-to-point commerce in ideas and data produced by ordinary businesses and individuals. Interactive banking is a simple example. Intel is pushing the technology, and this company's management is not waiting for the network medium to evolve. They are already proceeding. Consider this:

A familiar scene is enacted about a million times a day, and has been throughout human history: two people huddling over a complex piece of information. The practice may have begun with a pair of cavemen making plans for an animal hunt, scratching symbols and lines on the floor of a cave (beaters advance into the trees over here, so; spear throwers lie in wait behind these boulders, so).

In modern conferences the information is on paper. Thus, Napoleon and Ney huddle over the battle map of Austerlitz. Watson and Crick doodle chemical bonds on a napkin to sketch DNA. An accountant and a customer go over a tax form. Two executives scan a spreadsheet. A manager and foreman hammer out a schedule. An artist and a copywriter create a storyboard. An architect and a building contractor cost through a blueprint. A salesman and a purchasing agent review and negotiate price lists. Lawyers present contracts. Engineers unroll schematics. And so on exhaustively. The point is that in collaborative work, there is almost always a piece of paper on the tabletop between the two players.

This utterly simple scenario of two people putting their heads together over some information displayed on a tabletop is being strongly advanced by Intel Corporation as the basis for a new kind of business. But their idea is so very fundamental that it was, at first, slow to be comprehended.

Intel's new business concept is variously called desktop video teleconferencing and video telephony. They call it Indeo, a coinage that is evidently intended to marry the word *Intel* with the word *video*. But the idea is good. Say you are a building contractor. You are sitting at your personal computer. The phone rings, you answer. A small image of the caller, your plumbing subcontractor, appears in a window on your computer screen. It is superimposed on the upper left-hand corner of, say, a blueprint you are using to formulate a cost estimate. Simultaneously, on the caller's computer screen, a small image of you appears. So will the blueprint and, if you wish, parts of the tabulation of the estimate.

One of the things you must be able to do in a meeting is to single out items of importance by pointing at them. In PC video telephony there are no literal fingers, but you can indeed point at things, using mice and telecursors.

Upon its introduction, Intel's concept of meeting-by-computer was widely publicized and widely misunderstood.

The idea of conversing while being displayed on a screen embarrasses most people. But Intel's new technology does not merely provide a means for two heads to talk to each other on-camera. It includes something for them to talk about — the information on the computer screen. It could be a blueprint, a spreadsheet, a written document, a portfolio, a map, a schematic diagram, a schedule, a chemical cascade — virtually anything visual. The information on the screen corresponds to the information that, in a more traditional setting, would be spread out on a tabletop between two collaborators.

When Intel introduced the product, it was the little talking heads in windows that captured the attention of the media. It seemed a replay of the familiar science fiction set piece of video telephones, and this is how it was depicted on the evening TV news reports. But in Intel's concept, the computer is a complete medium for collaborating at a distance. It puts two heads together over a common working surface. Somehow, the all-important common working surface between the two people — the rest of the PC screen — was left out of the story the public was told. In effect, the received announcement of Intel's Indeo technology as a pure video telephone leaves Napoleon and Ney with no map spread between them, or Watson and Crick without their doodle of DNA. Patrick Gelsinger, who heads development of this project for Intel, expressed to me his frustration that Indeo was not better understood. "The data conferencing," he urges, "is far more important than the video."

The specific technology of Intel's PC conferencing system, as introduced, consisted of a little video camera that sits on top of the PC monitor, a pair of plug-in circuit boards, and an audio subsystem (headset, handset, or speakerphone). The introductory price was extremely aggressive at about $2,000. There are several public companies in the desktop videoconferencing business (Vtel, Compression Labs, PictureTel) and another twenty-two to twenty-five private companies either in the business or in the process of going into it. It is nevertheless a tiny field. Hambrecht and Quist analyst Randy Youen suggested that in its infancy, at year-end 1992, the total revenues for all participants was probably less that $20 million. It would appear that the sudden landing of Intel in this business atomized the prospects for many of the smaller companies who were hurrying into the field. But Youen has projected a business worth $2 billion by 1997.

This is only indirectly a hardware business for Intel. Their programmers are working to shift the lion's share of the task of video processing to the computer's CPU — that is, naturally, to the microprocessors that Intel manufactures. The processing task largely arises from the telephone network's limited capacity for data transmission.

A designated data line will realistically handle about 112 kilobits of data per second. Within this capacity limit, a sort of lowest common denominator, Intel allocates 14 kilobits for voice transmission, 10 kilobits for data (such as a shared spreadsheet), and 80 kilobits for the little video picture of you. This is not much of a bit budget. A single frame of the video is 120 pixels by 160 pixels, and each pixel represents 8 bits. Just one frame eats 153,600 bits. This is an excess of 40,000 bits over the total per-second capacity of the phone line.

To send your picture over the phone, the data stream that comprises your picture must be compressed at your end, crammed into the wire, and then decompressed for display at your collaborator's computer. It can be updated, or refreshed, at a rate of only twelve frames per second. The trick to video compression is to send down the wire only information that describes *changes* in the picture, not the whole picture. Your lips move — this is a change — but the bookcase and credenza behind you are static, and need not be repainted with every frame. Colors and lighting rarely change.

The greater the computational power brought to bear on the compression/decompression problem, the better the quality of the video. Let's put this in terms of processing power: mips, or millions of instructions per second. As the technology was being launched, an Intel 80486 processor running at 66 megahertz was good for 35 mips. Of the 35, according to Patrick Gelsinger, about 7 mips had to be dedicated to video compression and decompression. But processor power doubles every eighteen months. This means that in 1995, Patrick can focus 14 mips of processing power on his video task — doubling the quality of the picture.

In the year 2000, he'll have a 2-million-mips processor to play with, and this should deliver full-motion, full-frame video, with 60 percent of the mips left over to run applications. By that time, of course, the transmission paths really should be much wider, making the compression and decompression processing less arduous. Also by that time, competing processors will be running similar algorithms. But it helps to be first.

Intel is plainly forcing this technology, in the way a gardener might force a plant. Technically appropriate broadband telephone networks are not in place to support videoconferencing properly — they probably won't be for several years. But with cheap, massive processing power, Intel is promising to compute a way around the transmission bottleneck and turn video PC collaborations into an economically very productive commonplace.

By this means, interactive video via the nation's 200 million PCs will be a realistic possibility, certainly for businesses. The computers equipped for video telephony, most of them already hooked into corporate networks, will become magnets for the broadband cable networks of the future. It seems unlikely that two distinct and different networks will evolve — one for consumers, one for business — particularly when you consider the degree to which (given this specific Intel technology) business is going to be conducted from homes.

What seems likely is that the communication standards being worked out today for PC networks will become, by default, the compatibility standards for the information superhighway of the next decades.

How to invest? At this point, three overlaid networks are pulsing with promise: phone, cable, and satellite. Three is a testy number. Alliances are forming and dissolving. Two of the networks already have access to your house, and one (the phone company) has access to your workplace. On present information, there is no way to call a winner in this race — there probably will be no single winner or class of winners. Because the nets are already partly overlaid, it is doubtful that any new monopoly can be created, nor can an established monopoly be broken. The logical course is to hedge. Buy cable when it is down (for example, on news of failed acquisitions). Buy regional phone companies when *they* go down (for example, on news of impending acquisitions of cable companies).

And you might wish to buy a little fiber-optic stock. Corning makes it, for example. They are supplied in certain applications by a much smaller company, Spectran, which trades on the NASDAQ. The appeal of fiber optics is in its simplicity. Notice the heroic processing tasks associated with a simple exchange of pictures, data, and voice over wires and satellite links. For copper wires, the task is compression and decompression. For satellites, it is separation of signal from noise. For all three transmission media, there is encryption and decryption.

It strikes me as technically inelegant, a truly clunky piece of design, to use to its utmost our most complex, sophisticated silicon technology — the microprocessor — for a task that is so readily and easily accomplished by our simplest silicon technology, a glass wire. Technical aesthetics don't count for much in business, but simplicity certainly does, and fiber optics are simple. For this reason I am inclined to weight the bet toward stocks in those companies urging a fiber-optic network.

As for the satellite superhighway concept, there are no pure stock plays on it as yet.

As interactive technology develops, the test for investors will become simpler. We will need to ask in each instance, is this technology likely to produce a stream of recurring revenues? Equipment sells just once, so you should understand that if you invest in a manufacturer of hardware devices, such as video servers, you are buying into a boomlet and will need to take profits, rather than simply buy and hold. Software is fine if it is served over the networks, i.e., if it is to become a source of recurring revenues.

Finally, take your time. The future is a different place, once you get there, and this particular chunk of the future is rather dimly glimpsed at this early date.

Chapter 11

The Wireless Revolution?

THE INDUSTRIAL REVOLUTION was a revolution in mobility. People and goods were suddenly able to move far and fast. Distance dissolved, distant markets opened up. Suddenly, cattle raised in the Southwest and fattened in Illinois could be eaten in New York. Heavy machines constructed in Ohio were put to work in California. The economy itself was mobilized by technology. The mobility theme has since been replayed again and again in business: by the railroad barons, by Henry Ford, by Donald Douglas and his DC-3, by Soichiro Honda and his motorbikes. So deeply linked are the concepts of mobility and technological progress, historically, that we almost automatically assume that mobility makes money.

Telephone stocks are also hugely, vastly popular as investment instruments — perhaps the only individual stocks with mass-market appeal on a par with that of the mutual funds. Generations of Americans have confidently invested in telephone stock. Put telephony together with mobility and you have a virtually surefire stock promotion. Moreover, the concept has proved itself. In recent years many investors in the cellular phone stocks have been well rewarded. Is there any reason for these winners to question that the trick might not work once again for the latest generation of wireless phones? No, and one can guess from the frequent, abrupt runups in fashionable wireless stocks that few questions are being raised.

Similarly, the current generation of desktop computers is shadowed by a parallel generation of laptop, notebook, and pocket computers. The mobile computers are believed, by the industry, to be the highest growth market: computers to go. But go where?

Things really are changing. We will in a decade be far less mobile as a society because the economy will depend more on computers and less upon cars. Another decade beyond that and we may well have become practically sessile. When the upper tier of the economy is moving at the speed of light, which is the transmission speed of electronic information, then the advantages and thrills of moving people around at 65 or even 650 miles per hour will have been largely trivialized. The big drag on the economy will have become freight transport: the rate at which tangibles — goods — can be shifted from point to point. The less passenger traffic, of course, the more rapidly the freight-carrying networks and conduits will be able to deliver.

When the 1994 earthquake in Los Angeles diced the city's famous network of freeways, and people could not drive to work, quite a few of them were able to work from home via computer links. In this emergency, the communication network was able to assume some of the burden of the failed transportation network. And where wired communications broke down, wireless phones filled in.

This turns out to be a pretty strong metaphor for what is happening to the civilization. The transportation system has essentially failed. Too many people have too many different places to go. Traffic is becoming impossible.

It seems clear that over time, communication will outperform passenger transportation as a commercial pursuit. This is because communication is steadily supplanting transportation as a productive thing to do. For example, the difference between commuting by car or train and telecommuting by computer is vast. You walk from the breakfast table to the computer and flip it on. Now you're working. Hours are saved. Much petroleum is left uncombusted. Lives are saved. And so on.

What will become of the mobile phone and the portable computer in a sessile society? What will happen to the market for these products when, as we happily drive our computers to work, our cars sit cold in their garages?

Perhaps that day is many years away. In the meantime, there is no question that the mobility-enhancing products are going to have a pretty nice little run. But will the stocks? Not many. The danger to investors is not obsolescence: it is commoditization in telecommunications generally. This means the products and services are becoming essentially identical in their features. They must increasingly compete on price. Multiple communication networks are overlaying each other, and for this reason they are losing their essential money-making quality — protected access.

Recall the pattern of the commercial history of railway networks, or the more recent decline into unprofitability of the airline industry. Whenever the pioneering, proprietary hub-and-spokes networks are overlaid on each other, through growth, intersections between networks are opened up. At each intersecting line, customers suddenly have choices between two proprietary networks' services. Competition arises, prices sink.

Eventually the highly profitable hub-and-spokes patterns merge into a centerless, nationwide Cartesian grid. As the original centers disappear, the potential for extraordinary profit is forever lost. The emergence of multiple wireless access paths to the major wired networks looks suspiciously like the beginnings of a Cartesian grid, a supernet, and the beginning of the end of extraordinary or even very consistent profits from telecommunications.

To pick stocks in this area, look for monopoly breakers, rather than monopoly makers. The era of telecommunication monopolies is almost past. Eventually telecommunication services will have to compete primarily on price. Commoditization ultimately depresses margins, earnings, and stock prices. The portable laptop and notebook computers are already commoditized, and their profit margins will naturally decline with time. Note too the price collapse in cellular phones. This is what wireless really seems to add up to: it is at bottom more a story about competition than mobility.

There are five major types of wireless telecommunication techniques attracting interest from investors: the familiar and well-established cellular telephony networks; the conventional radio telephony dispatch systems long used by cabs and industry; a new "PCS" standard network for small messaging computers such as the Apple Newton; the already established wireless data networks of Ardis, BellSouth, and Ram Broadcasting; and satellite links.

To begin sorting this out, note the most obvious thing first: there are many different ways to communicate without wires. Theoretically, pathways through the air can be created instantaneously between any two points, or between any one point and many others. Because they can be made to exist instantly, by switching on a transmitter, wireless networks seem fundamentally unlike railway, roadway, canal, coaxial, copper wire, tower microwave, or fiber-optic networks — any of which may require years of capital- and labor-intensive efforts to physically put into place.

It would appear from the chosen name — wireless — that the radiotelephone communication technologies are potentially monopoly breakers, since they could in principle bypass the wired telephone networks to directly reach a captive customer base. But to break a monopoly you must bypass it altogether. All wireless can accomplish at this point is to open up points of access to the existing wired networks. With the exception of some satellite-based technologies, the wireless communication devices are low-powered and have only a short working range.

For example, the cellular, PCS, and RAM broadcasting radio links all work by transmitting from a portable phone or a portable computer to a relay or transfer station. From that point, the message goes by telephone wire. The revenues produced by a "wireless phone" call are thus shared by the wireless company and the wired telephone company. In other words, most of the so-called wireless systems are really cordless systems. They transmit only as far as that nearby point where the wires begin.

It is easy to visualize a futuristic long-distance call directly linking any two wireless phones — and thus bypassing all the networks and their fees. The cost to the callers would come down to the irreducible minimum, which is just the cost of the wattage of their signals, i.e., the cost of electricity. Ham radio operators have communicated in this way for many decades. But a direct wireless phone system would not be commercially intriguing to any corporation, or a long-term good investment, because it would be an open-access system. It would also, unfortunately, clog the airways to a degree that would probably make it impractical.

A geometric, point-to-point, commercially practical version of such a direct wireless phone system can and probably will be created using relay satellites — but this concept puts us right back into a controlled-access network with high capital cost. Motorola owns 34 percent of Iridium, Inc., an international consortium building a $3.37 billion satellite phone system. Ultimately the system will comprise sixty-six satellites. An alternative system is to be lofted by Comsat in conjunction with another international consortium. A third, low-orbit satellite system for broadband super-high-frequency transmission has been proposed to the FCC. High-profile participants in this network, designed by a company called Teledesic, include Microsoft's Bill Gates and McCaw Cellular's Craig McCaw.

However, by the time the overhead networks are shot into orbit, customers on the ground will have many alternative pathways for communicating, including switchable broadband cables. Skeptics have suggested that for this reason, the profitability of the various satellite systems may never add up to much. The satellite nets are perhaps conceived as bypass networks — data railroads speeding past the ground-bound data barge canals, stealing the whole business. We know that radio can indeed reach past wires to open up a formerly captive customer base. But there seems to be no overwhelming advantage in a satellite network's speed or capacity. The bandwidth is an awesome 30 gigahertz, but a competitive system can probably be achieved less expensively with fiber optics. The customers on the ground are not captive, so the business does not have the built-in commercial energy of a monopoly breaker. And satellites are *très* expensive. Teledesic, with 840 satellites, needs at least $9 billion up front.

It does seem almost inevitable that someday, geographically remote wireless cells will find ways to intercommunicate by bypassing or at least minimizing the involvement of wired networks on which they now depend. The simplest way to do it would be by forming a cellular cooperative and stringing some wires to interconnect remote cells. Another, similar idea is to bypass cellular and use radiotelephones for local service and microwave or hardwire links for long distance. MCI is well equipped to accomplish this, and they certainly know it. The eventual remarriage of local and long-distance telephone services will not be a commercial or technical breakthrough, however. It is likely that it will simply complete the commoditization of the telecommunications business.

So far, today's commercial wireless isn't even wireless. What it provides is access, from a hand-held or dash-mounted portable radio transceiver, to the established, extensively wired telephone networks. For this reason the revenues from most wireless services must be split with a wired network. Thus, the profit margins of wireless are, from the outset, banging against an inherently low ceiling.

Not only has this alarmed the companies developing and selling "wireless" services, it has sharply aroused the interest, competitive zeal, and perhaps the ire of the wired carriers. For them, outside avenues of access to their wired networks bleed off profits that might have been theirs exclusively. In other words, wireless is opening side-door access conduits to the major wired telephone systems. In major East Coast markets, for example, Bell Atlantic, the wired network, must share revenue on cellular calls with Southwestern Bell, which is, in this territory, an interloping provider of wireless cellular services.

The major common carriers are quickly (one might even say hastily) buying into wireless services they can offer under their own auspices. MCI, AT&T, and many of the so-called Baby Bells have made steps in this direction. MCI was particularly aggressive. It nearly acquired 17 percent of a wireless company, Nextel, an investment valued at $1.3 billion, but the deal fell apart. AT&T offered close to $18 billion to acquire McCaw Cellular Communications. With wireless, the long-distance carriers can spread their fingers into lucrative local metropolitan markets currently dominated by the Baby Bells.

At the same time, and as a counterattack on the long-distance carriers, the regional Bell companies are also going into wireless and are seeking to sell long-distance services. Can any of these interests, reaching across each other's face to get at their respective customers, hope to recreate some sort of grand old phone company monopoly? Absolutely not. Telecommunications is becoming a wildly competitive arena. It will never again sustain a major nationwide monopoly.

What about wireless from a technology standpoint? Technology is a secondary consideration, but there is a progression in age from oldest to youngest, and a corresponding progression in transmission modes from analog to digital. The oldest wireless approach is that of Nextel, and it is the familiar two-way communication system used for many years for dispatching taxis and other fleet vehicles.

(We used to call such devices radios, of course. The regression to the more archaic term *wireless* is evidently intended to underline the phones' mobility.)

A newer but also well-established wireless technique is the cellular telephone. There are two kinds of cellular phone — analog and digital. Analog cellular phone calls are readily intercepted. In fact, eavesdropping has become a popular public pastime. Phone monitoring equipment is sold through enthusiast magazines and by mail to hobbyists, and professional-level equipment is manufactured for the use of detectives, police, and other licensed snoops. Digital cellular phones, which are newer, are much harder to listen in on, because the voice input signals are converted to a digital bit stream and can be encrypted before transmission.

The still more recent approach is PCS, for "personal communications services." PCS is basically cellular technology by another name, written smaller. In a cellular network, the cells, which are areas served by stations that convey the wireless messages into telephone wires, are five to ten miles apart. Cells are much smaller in the PCS mode than in cellular telephony — the PCS cells are in fact called microcells, and in some cases may be just a few hundred feet apart. Transmission is digital, and the PCS medium is attractive not just for phones but for wireless computing as well. This is partly because PCS operates at extremely high frequencies, 1.8 gigahertz, which is double that of cellular phones. This means PCS can rapidly transfer a heavy burden of digital data from one computer to another. Apple's famous Newton and other hand-held computing devices can use PCS to its best advantage.

On purely technical grounds, because of its broader bandwidth, PCS seems favored to emerge as the winning technology, but this is hardly an issue a technology can win. FCC regulators have stipulated that in cellular phone markets, there must be two service suppliers — but in PCS markets, the number of competitors is to be seven. Whether or not this level of competition can be sustained (one cannot legislate survival), it points in the direction things are going.

Phone company profits have always arisen from regulated monopolies, not technologies. The wireless explosion is another step, perhaps the last one, toward commoditization of this field. In other words, wireless is not a gold mine. It is a gold rush, which is a whole lot less profitable as a long-term investment concept. In the short and intermediate term the most conservative approach would probably be to buy stock in Motorola.

This company has put itself into a diverse portfolio of wireless technologies. It is widely thought among investors that this will assure Motorola's ascendency in whichever wireless mode emerges as dominant. But it is quite possible that none will emerge as dominant, in which case Motorola can benefit to some degree from most of their many competing technologies. More speculative investors might wish to take a look at Qualcomm, a San Diego firm that owns patents on an attractive multiplexing technology. It has the effect of multiplying the service capacity of a cellular network.

Qualcomm has in addition an established and profitable business with the trucking industry, using satellite radio to communicate with and report on the positions of trucks and their freight in transit on the highways. Both these stocks are technologically hedged, and in examining wireless stocks in general this is a quality you should look for. As for the telecommunications networks, wired and wireless, I would avoid taking positions in their stocks except as short-to-intermediate-term trading plays, mostly on specific acquisitions.

Some investors have had some success at finding a replay of the past glory of the telephone business by purchasing telephone stocks in foreign countries where the phone companies are indeed funded with stock, rather than owned outright by the government. But I think one can discover more secure and reliable networks to invest in by looking ahead. Nostalgia is not a strategy.

Chapter 12

Computers, Semiconductors, and Eternal Youth

THE IMAGE OF HIGH TECHNOLOGY as something glorious and special was formed in the 1960s and 1970s around the spectacular success of the semiconductor industry. The history of the industry's pioneering integrated circuit makers is simple to tell.

They found a way to reproduce electronic circuits photographically.

To manufacture circuits in a factory once required hundreds of assemblers and binsful of discrete electronic components (capacitors, resistors, transistors) and intensive, squinting, meticulous labor. It took acres of space and man-years of time to do basic electronic circuit manufacturing. But with the progress of the semiconductor industry, this entire manufacturing enterprise was reduced to photography. Click. Done. A snapshot.

Photographically, a circuit of enormous complexity can be reproduced just as easily as a simple circuit. It does not require a bigger plant or a larger team of assemblers or more time.

The cost of complexity therefore dived. The size of a circuit reproduced photographically can be reduced photographically, and so the physical size of electronic circuits was also reduced fantastically in the 1960s and 1970s. Progress since has been more difficult but dramatic nevertheless.

As semiconductor technology has matured, it has absorbed more and more of the electronic manufacturing business. The process is called integration, and its emblem and talisman is the integrated circuit. Eventually, the semiconductor industry will sponge up the entire electronic manufacturing process. Consider the effects of this in, for example, the computer field.

There is today very little value left to be added by computer manufacturers. They buy a big chip and they stick it in a socket. Famous everlasting price wars between computer manufacturers have obscured the real underlying transformation of their business. At this point many computer manufacturers have become packaging and retailing outlets for Intel and Motorola. Discount retailers at that.

Because the semiconductor business has subsumed the business of building computers, the computer manufacturing business per se is over. Those companies still calling themselves computer manufacturers seem to succeed to the extent that they have transformed themselves into de facto software and semiconductor companies. I know of only one computer company that understood this view of itself and its market. It was Apple. Apple was a software company of the first rank. When it surrendered its leadership role in software to Microsoft, it lost its way completely.

Semiconductor companies are well positioned to pick up the markets dropped by failing computer companies. Micron Technologies, a colorful Idaho maverick among semiconductor companies, noticed there was no very good reason not to go into the computer business — and did it. As a memory manufacturer, Micron is able to keep its cost of goods low on one of the more expensive components of modern desktop computers, the memory chips. Because of the massively increasing use of pictorial programs, contemporary computers consume heroic quantities of memory chips. As a memory maker, Micron is well positioned to develop a cost-cutting edge in the commodity desktop computer business, where more memory and a lower price are two of the most important ways to distinguish one's product.

As the computer business has evolved into a semiconductor business, most major computer companies are backstopping themselves by developing or reemphasizing their own semiconductor capabilities. At this writing, Digital Equipment manufactures the fastest microprocessor available, which they call Alpha. IBM has long been a significant semiconductor manufacturer. Ditto Sun Microsystems. With IBM and Motorola, Apple has collaborated in the development of the PowerPC microprocessor. Compaq is a significant investor in a semiconductor company that is offering workalike clones of Intel microprocessors. Through these arrangements, the computer manufacturers can hope to reclaim the profitability, and the technological content, of the computer business.

At fifty, the semiconductor industry is straining a bit to maintain its image as a hyperenergetic California adolescent. It is in fact a mature multinational industry and should be evaluated by investors using yardsticks reserved for mature industrial stocks. Watch its margins, dividends, and payout ratios — and don't expect remarkable growth or revolutionary progress. Semiconductors are a cyclic and technologically predictable product. They get smaller, faster, and cheaper. There is a splendid giant in the business, Intel. It is a monopoly under siege, but then monopolies are always under siege. It is still a good core holding. Motorola is similarly attractive. But having said this, there is little more to be said.

So, is the semiconductor revolution over? Maybe not.

There has emerged in the past two decades a broad new class of semiconductors that can be programmed in the most basic way: they can be wired and even rewired in place. The consequences for investors are important.

The first changeable chips were used as prototyping "breadboard" tools by engineers. Say a hardware designer wanted to try out a particular chip circuit — without spending three or four months and $100,000 in engineering costs to set up a chip fabrication line for his experimental circuit design. The ideal answer would be a "blank" chip. Such chips can be reconfigured — wired for a specific task — with special chip programming equipment provided by their manufacturers. The engineer could try out a design inexpensively with just one or two of these special, changeable chips. Concept to prototype would take just four days. Then, if the specially configured chip performed as intended, it would be safe to commit capital to make a production run of conventionally manufactured semiconductors.

As the cost of changeable chips has dropped, it has become realistic to push them forward from prototyping to production. The customized chip is sold as the manufacturer's own product, at least for a while, and the value is added to the chip by simply configuring (i.e., wiring) it for an intended task, rather than by manufacturing it from scratch. If it seems that the circuit will have a long season, the manufacturer may ultimately risk a run of dedicated chips. But increasingly, the product simply evolves without ever being frozen into a single design.

Computer product cycles have grown shorter and shorter. Consider how rapidly the Intel generations progressed from the 8088 to the 8086, the 80286, the 80386, the 80486, the Pentium, and so on. It has made excellent sense to many manufacturers of the surrounding circuitry and accessory boards to keep up with this generational Ferris wheel by specifying mutable chips; the alternative would have been to go through a rapid-fire succession of costly retoolings for each and every product generation.

An important general idea for technology investors is to watch closely for companies that can profit by technological change rather than be swept aside by it. The concept of changeable chips is almost a paradigm for this type of business.

One example is Xilinx Corporation. This company manufactures chips that can be configured as desired by other manufacturers. Xilinx sells, additionally, the software and hardware its customers can use to do the configuring. With the delivery of this equipment comes a culture, a technology, a language. Once it is installed the customer's engineers and logic designers and production people become expert at using it. In this way the Xilinx approach to making circuits is woven into and through its customers' businesses. The Xilinx technology can also migrate, as an expertise acquired by its customers' people, to other plants and other applications. The Xilinx culture both locks up existing business and brings in new business, and so this culture is the company's real product. The follow-on products, the blank chip, the raw material, is consumed by this culture as blades are consumed by razors. Between October 1990, at a low following the invasion of Kuwait, and March 1994, Xilinx appreciated sixfold. For a $1,000 investment, a $5,000 return in somewhat less than four years.

Lattice Semiconductor has an even more interesting programmable chip. This is because it can be configured not only as a specific electronic product — it can be reconfigured after the fact. With Lattice's electronically reprogrammable chips, the circuit designer can try one design, erase it, and then try another. For some of Lattice's chips, this can be accomplished without even removing the device from its mount on a circuit board.

For Lattice's customers, who sell electronics, this means that a chip that is not quite right can be remanufactured in place to correct problems or add new features. What it means to the computer, semiconductor, and electronic manufacturing business in the future is perhaps more profoundly important.

If you could upgrade your computer to the more advanced technology of the latest model *electronically* — would you ever buy a new one? Suppose you could accomplish such an upgrade over the telephone, via modem. A nice convenience. To trade up to this year's hot new computer, just call for a download. The idea gives a new meaning to the popular concept of shopping by phone.

This maturing technology underlines a point that can be made in many ways. The computer, semiconductor, and electronic hardware businesses are evolving away from manufacturing itself. Ultimately these businesses will be services — software services — and this is primarily where their profits will arise. Lattice's stock is a good way to invest in this transition.

Lattice is an attractive long-term stock for another reason. It is peripherally involved in the field of video scrambling. Its chips are sentinels guarding the cable boxes in the homes of cable television subscribers. The chip must be configured in a certain way for the descrambler box to work. Cable service operators reconfigure the Lattice chip from time to time to foil video thieves. This chip is essentially rewired by the cable company, remotely, by sending appropriate signals over the system.

Conventional video scrambling is at the pioneering level of a very important business, broadly characterized as encryption. This chiefly means, to investors, the protection of access to commercially valuable information products through the mechanism of encoding.

Here is a fencing technology. It has the power to turn a company that is now only marginally profitable (for example, a company in the software business) into a solidly paying proposition. Encryption accomplishes this by building a fence around a product or network.

To see the magnitude of the market for encryption, consider the practice of "hacking," that is, gaining illegal access to phones, private faxes, computer networks and software, TV shows and movies, private conversations, and electronic funds transfers. Begin with cellular phones, an easy target.

Eavesdropping on a cellular telephone conversation is, in the United States, a federal crime punishable by five years of imprisonment and/or a $250,000 fine. So you mustn't ever do it. But the law is so easy to break, you might just break it by accident. You might, for example, simply tune an old TV set through the upper UHF channels; cellular phone conversations are there to be heard.

A slightly more sophisticated wireless wiretapper might purchase a scanner radio through the electronic hobbyists' magazines; this does a much more workmanlike job of eavesdropping. Devices for sale by mail can detect the phone numbers, and thus the identities, of the conversationalists. This is one reason you should never convey your credit card numbers over a wireless phone. The bottom line is, the law against tapping a cellular phone is about as enforceable as the famous and famously lampooned law against removing mattress tags.

As the country shifts to digital wireless phones the problem will change, but digitizing is not enough. Digitally encoded voice messages (like fax transmissions) are conveyed as streams of ones and zeros, rather than recognizable voices, but they can readily be intercepted and turned back into voices by any appropriate digital phone receiver — just as any ordinary fax machine can make sense of any fax transmission. Digital transmissions are, however, easy to render into secret code. It just requires an encryption chip.

The idea of encoding electronic signals to protect commercial products from electronic theft is not limited to phones, faxes, and data transmission. Cable TV companies routinely protect access to their networks through a variety of electronic scrambling and descrambling schemes. Software manufacturers have long attempted, with mixed success, to encode their programs in such a way as to restrict their use to legitimate purchasers and to frustrate the circulation of "free" copies.

Commercial and government satellites use elaborate encryption technologies to prevent signal theft or remote seizure of command of the satellite's systems. Government satellites' downlinks and uplinks are among the best-protected communication channels in history. Mycotronyx began as a small privately held software company in Torrance, California. It has a substantial specialized business in encryption for satellites and is helping to bring this government technology out into the commercial marketplace. In 1994, Mycotronyx was acquired by a NASDAQ–listed company, Rainbow Technology.

An early application will be in encryption for secure phone, fax, and data transmissions, with other, follow-on applications in such security-sensitive areas as electronic funds transfer. Mycotronyx's technical partner in this work is VLSI Technology, Inc., of San Jose. VLSI is a publicly traded stock and is one attractive way to invest in encryption technology. VLSI has devised an encryption chip so secure that a cipher key cannot be read out of it, even if it is sliced open and examined under a scanning electron microscope. Some other plays on the encryption theme are Lattice Semiconductor, whose chips help secure access to cable TV; Advanced Micro Devices; and Xilinx.

The field of encryption using government-standard coding algorithms has been absurdly politicized. This is because the specific encryption standards urged by the government are, by definition, decipherable by government law enforcement agencies such as the FBI.

Opponents of encryption to the government's standard are quick to raise the specter of Big Brother. Skeptics argue that the bad guys will develop their own ciphers to thwart eavesdropping by the FBI — as of course they will. Critics also argue that the government's code, like every other code, can be cracked. This is also true.

But the issue is still trivial. Encryption is coming. It will come in one form or another — it is already here in diverse forms — because it is a commercial necessity. When a business puts something of value onto the public wires or airwaves, be it a conversation about a customer, a TV show, a computer program or, most critically, an electronic transfer of funds, it should be protected by encryption.

There are degrees of security. The idea is to raise a fence against product theft just high enough that it is cheaper to pay for the product (i.e., the movie, the computer program) than to take the time and shoulder the expense of hacking the code. To hack one "node" of a network protected with the VLSI chips — say, just one cable TV box — allow about half a million dollars. (For a satellite, write your hackers' budget in billions and decades.)

VLSI has taken an early lead in encryption chips, and they offer some proprietary technology, particularly for extremely sensitive applications. They estimate the value of the various markets for their particular encryption technology at $100 million over the span of three years, though there is no way to guess how much of this market they can actually capture.

Encryption is a transforming technology in several important ways. It is possible that it can transform the software business into a more profitable pursuit by erecting around it, at long last, Richard Trevithick's famous fence. A highly developed software package is not less sophisticated, as a piece of engineering, than the Brooklyn Bridge. Yet the whole program — representing an investment of years of work — can be stolen in about a minute by simply copying it to a floppy disk. Software manufacturers estimate that as many as four-fifths of the running copies of their programs are illicit freebies.

Encryption alone cannot protect software. There have been many such schemes, and they have all essentially failed. A combination of encryption and semiconductor hardware works a little better, however. Suppliers of custom programs now typically supply along with them a hardware key. This is a plug-in device containing a chip, and programmed onto the chip is a unique code number. The key must be inserted into a standard socket supplied on the back panel of every desktop computer.

Before the protected program will run, it "looks" to this socket for the passcode number. The program will not run unless the key is plugged in. And only one key is provided with each copy of the program. The key can be defeated, but, because it is hardware, cannot be easily counterfeited. This technology was pioneered by Rainbow Technologies, but is available now from several sources. It works because it makes it cheaper and easier to buy the program than to copy it. Some software companies and at least one semiconductor company have raised the idea of incorporating a permanent ID chip on the mother board of every computer. Software could then be configured by the seller to "look for" this chip.

None of this is tamperproof. Once any computer program has been uploaded into memory, it can be downloaded to a floppy by a knowledgeable thief. But knowledgeable thieves are not the problem. The problem is casual copying by ordinary computerists.

In yet another approach to commercial software protection, encryption is also combined with hardware, but the hardware element is more traditional: it is a network. In this schema, software is never distributed for sale at all. It is simply maintained at a hub, and the product for sale is whatever service it performs. Encrypted data traverse the network. The software receives them, operates on them, and returns them. Questions come in, answers go out. Because the software is never delivered, it can never be copied.

Portfolio analysis services already operate in this way. Modem in a list of your stocks — back comes a list of what to sell and what to keep.

The program cannot be freely copied by customers because they never get their hands on it. Instead of a one-shot sale, the software company receives a recurring stream of revenues for services performed. On a small scale, network-based software can be secured and sold as a service by installing it only on the central servers of local- and wide-area networks within large companies. In a way, this replicates the old hub-and-spokes patterns of the mainframe and minicomputer networks of the 1960s and 1970s. But in this plan, the proprietary control of the hub is inherent in the software rather than the hardware.

To make centralized software work as a nationwide marketing approach, the incoming and outgoing private data must be encrypted, and computer networks must become (as they are in fact becoming) more accessible and pervasive.

Lotus Development, now a division of IBM, pioneered the selling of software as a service through an agreement with AT&T to market Lotus's Notes program. When the agreement was announced, it was as though someone had struck a gigantic Chinese gong. Everyone in the industry and in the stock market suddenly started paying attention. Novell, perhaps too late, expressed great interest in the same type of marketing method as a way to resist or reverse the commoditization of the packaged-software business.

The future of this business pivots, as do so many other information- and technology-based businesses, upon encryption. Encryption technology itself consists of mathematical algorithms that are largely made available for free by the U.S. government. As public property, they hold no interest for investors. The specialized semiconductors that do the work of encryption and decryption do offer attractive investments. Many specialized chips have, in the past, found their markets undermined by microprocessors. As microprocessors have grown more powerful, they have increasingly taken on tasks formerly relegated to specialty chips. The trade term for this is *migration to the microprocessor.*

Most recently, it has affected the market for specialty chips that accomplish compression and decompression of video signals for transmission over the telephone. Intel, as a seller of microprocessors, naturally wishes to absorb this piece of business into future generations of microprocessors. Will the same thing happen to encryption? Maybe not. Some encryption chips contain special technology designed to frustrate the intelligence-gathering efforts of hostile governments. This same technology tends to protect the security chips as a specialized business. If encryption should migrate to the micro-processor, a level of security would be lost. Encryption chips may even grab some of the microprocessor business, which is, after all, hardly sacrosanct. One VLSI encryption chip actually contains, as an embedded accessory item, a 32-bit microprocessor, and this is not an unusual practice.

Chapter 13

When Software
Was Harder

SOFTWARE IS SUPPOSED to simplify life — to make it quick and easy to accomplish things that used to be complicated and difficult. Ironically, computer software is itself widely criticized for being complicated and hard to learn. Word processors in particular have often been parodied for their command languages — obscure gibberish that must be invoked to accomplish the simplest everyday tasks.

Why is this? Programmers work naturally in code. It is their metier. When the thinking of the programmer surfaces — becomes visible to the computer user, in an on-screen instruction or in a required command — it tends to reveal itself as deeply encoded, nested, involute.

This seems like an easy problem to solve. Programs can be made understandable to ordinary people by getting ordinary people involved in the software development process, in focus groups and in beta-testing programs. Yet the gibberish — the computerese of computer programs — persists. Again, why?

Bear in mind that the business of computer software has not been based, historically, on making things simple. It has been based on keeping things difficult. In the first decades of the computer industry, computer software was wholly incomprehensible to the people who most needed the answers a computer could provide: accountants, financial analysts, inventory managers, et al.

Programmers in that benighted era assumed the role of an ancient oracular priest class — putting questions to the computer on behalf of mere mortals who came (humbly) to ask it this and that. Needless to say, it was the priests who specified purchasing requirements for computers and software, and the computer vendors thus developed a vested interest in the perpetuation of this class — and of the grand gibberish of data processing.

This is not a new pattern. Analogies can be seen in the relationship of physicians and pharmaceutical companies. A shared and specialized knowledge, specialized products, and specialized language all add up to a very secure and well-protected drug business. Similarly, the monopoly of lawyers is based on specialized knowledge and an obscurantist language.

The oracular culture in the computer business began to break down with the advent of desktop computers. It is understating the case to say that these little machines, which made computer power freely accessible to anyone, were not at first welcomed in corporate environments.

The reason early desktop computers were manufactured by Compaq as portables (luggables, they were called at the time) was essentially military. The idea was to mount a physical invasion of the corporate culture. The little computers had to be carried into the corporations, by hand, by revolutionaries. (Such as they were. MBAs.) Established corporate computing people, circled round their minis and mainframes, fighting for their importance, did not welcome this challenge to their power.

In the desktop culture, analogies were freely drawn to political revolutions — less often but not uncommonly to the Reformation. The Bible, once reserved to a priest class educated in its specialized (Latin) language, was translated into common English and made widely available by the new technology of the printing press. Translators were caught and burned at the stake, but they were many and they ultimately prevailed. The King James Bible became a mass-market item accessible to anyone who could read plain English. The analogy to the Reformation is remarkably complete — so complete that the best investment guide to the software business is probably *With Bible and Sword*, Barbara Tuchman's marvelous account of the

Reformation. But the reformation of the computer business remains unfinished.

The desktop computer revolution went the way of many a Latin American coup. The revolutionaries, having seized power, quickly turned rotten — they ended up just as bad as the establishment they had toppled. In the early 1980s a new priest class grew up around the desktops and the new software that ran on them. The software (spreadsheets, databases, word processors) was not manifested in plain English after all. It required training classes, technical support, and gurus within corporations who could solve problems for hesitant neophyte computerists.

Not surprisingly, the new gurus began to specify purchases for hardware and software; they developed relationships with the vendors; and the business arrived back where it started. The players were different, but the business depended once again on things being difficult and staying difficult — on specialized knowledge and specialized languages. And on priests.

If you learned Lotus 1-2-3, or dBASE, or WordPerfect, you would invest quite a bit of time in this process — and you would become a loyal user of the product. Your loyalty followed from the fact that the product was hard to use. You would not want to trouble yourself to learn another such program. So you kept using Lotus, and recommending it to your co-workers, and buying the name-branded upgrades. What did this mean from a business and investment standpoint?

It meant that a generation of software monopolies, created in the 1980s, was built around hard-to-use software. A software product such as WordPerfect became a cult, a cabal, complete with secret codes and hand signals. It perpetuated itself and the software business that supported it.

In other words, the software game consisted of introducing products that were advertised as easy to use but were actually hard to use — because the difficulty of learning these programs helped the software business sustain itself. Software was not sold as a product but as a culture, supported by training programs, special codes and languages, and by the customers' investments in past training and experience. It wove itself into the customers' corporate structures.

But what happened when software appeared that really *was* easy to use? All hell broke loose.

In one year, 1992, net profit margins in packaged software

dropped from 25 percent to 5 percent. The stocks also plummeted. Serious questions were raised about the ultimate survival of many of the software houses. Most of them failed or merged. The reason is Microsoft's Windows. Windows was the King James Bible of the software business.

It accomplishes two things. First, it defines a "standard interface," that is, a simple look. Every program that runs under Windows has this same look — and works the same way. If you have learned to use one such program, you have learned to use them all. In other words, competitive products are readily interchangeable. With the introduction of competition, software prices have faltered. In an extreme example, a program costing $795 in 1991 could be purchased for $95 in 1992.

Second, programs that run under Windows do not rely much on menus or coded special commands, as of old. Instead they use pushbuttons. Arrays of these buttons appear on the screen. A mouse is used to position a cursor over the button. When the mouse is clicked, the button on the screen appears to be depressed — just as though it had been pushed with a fingertip. Everyone knows how to push a button. Each one is clearly labeled, usually with a picture depicting its purpose. (To print a page, for example, you might depress a button emblazoned with a tiny picture of a printer.)

You might well ask, why not provide a manufactured keyboard with real pushbuttons, duly labeled? The earliest word processing machines actually did this. They had the complicated keyboards of a great organ. For a desktop computer, however, which must run many different kinds of programs, multiple specialized keyboards would be required, and this is impractical. Windows programs solve the problem by creating, on the screen, any pushbuttons that are needed by the program. For other tasks, the program can erase a set of buttons and put different buttons onto the screen.

This is the real meaning of Windows, and of the current generation of computers with their graphical user interfaces: pushbuttons. Programs that can be learned without training. And the demolition of product cultures and monopolies based on difficult-to-use software. The Reformation is finally here.

What does it mean to investors? It means that an era of high profit margins is past. To make money on packaged software stocks, you must now concentrate on trading them. Don't buy any packaged software stock with the intention of holding it. Ignore technology features. Buy and sell on technical signals. Pay attention to the company's gifts for advertising, marketing, litigating, packaging, and merchandising. The software business is evolving into a par product competition, like that of airlines. It is marketing and pricing, not technology, that can now distinguish one packaged software company and product over another.

Fortunately for investors, not all software comes in packages. High profit margins and good new markets still exist for many specialized software companies, as we shall see.

Chapter 14

The Electric Teacher

IN THE REMOTE, cold, copper-smelting town of Monche-gorsk, Russia, about one hundred miles south of the port city of Murmansk, schoolchildren in a public classroom are very rapidly learning to speak English from specialized computers.

These machines, which were developed by a tiny company, Boswell International in Vancouver, British Columbia, are equipped with voice synthesis chips that give them the power of speech. Digitally synthesized voice chips and a specialized keyboard, coupled with the computer's familiar power to fetch and display text and images, has kicked the technology of teaching English to a new high level. Users have nicknamed the machine "the Boswell." Comparative studies conducted in Canada suggest it teaches English five times faster than the best conventional methods, including fully equipped language laboratories of the old, familiar record/playback style.

A picture dictionary is built into the Boswell, and the computer does things no human language teacher could ever do. For example, to illustrate the sound of a *T*, in response to a single keystroke, the computer displays an animated cutaway image of the tongue touching the upper palate in just the right spot. The sound system makes the sound of *T* and simultaneously, synchronously shows the student how to do it. Text examples of *T*-words are displayed on the screen and repeated by the voice chip as exercises. The Boswell can repeat this animated, orchestrated, and textual presentation of *T* every single time the key is pressed — an infinite number of times — at the discretion of the student. The machine is, of course, tireless. It is never bored. It never signals to the student, however subtly, a message of impatience or discouragement.

The Boswells of Monchegorsk were installed as a public service by Minproc Engineers, Inc., an American company based in Englewood, Colorado, that does business with the copper industry in the town. This splendidly conceived gift builds goodwill and cultural bridges at the same time. It is also an excellent demonstration of the power of computerized instruction. Note that the Russian children are learning from the machines not just a new language but a new and, to them, unfamiliar alphabet. (A tough nut. Imagine yourself attempting to read their Cyrillic alphabet.) And they are receiving a level of instruction that would be impossible to replicate in Monchegorsk using human English teachers. In post-cold-war Russia, resources for schools (teachers, money, time) are all scarce. At reasonable cost, the computer provides to many children the intensive, completely personalized instruction that might be demanded of a private tutor to a single child born to great privilege. Learning from a computer is, in some respects, like going to Oxford. The ratio of students to teachers is unity: one on one.

It is no accident that the Boswell technology was developed in Vancouver, probably the most Asian city in North America, with a vigorous trading economy that looks to the Pacific Rim and a rapidly growing immigrant population of Asian Canadians who want to learn English. The Boswell was first conceived and developed in a collaboration between a court reporter and a language professor. The use of the specialized keyboard is the first thing the machine teaches the student. Press any key — watch and listen. The process of learning to use the machine's special keyboard takes fifty minutes or less. From that point on, the student is learning the English language.

The first significant sales of the Boswell were to a small Vancouver employment agency — a business with a bluntly economic purpose in mind. They wanted to teach immigrants basic English quickly — and just enough English to make them employable at a menial level, as janitors, for instance. The idea was to teach words like *on, off, stop, sweep, exit, danger.*

It turned out, of course, that with the Boswell, the students could manage much more. The more they learned, the greater their personal marketability in their new country. As the Boswell has caught on, banks of them have been installed by employers in manufacturing plants — for training, but also as a perk or added incentive. Employees are encouraged to use them free on their own time to improve their English, and they do so at every opportunity.

Boswell International has also actively developed its business overseas, and sells the machine via agents into China, Hong Kong, Korea, and throughout the Far East. The interest in Asia comes from executives in companies and institutions who do business with North America and want to pick up English as a marketing and negotiating tool. Note that in the Far East, as in Monchegorsk, it is not merely a language but also a wholly foreign alphabet that must be conveyed to the students.

Boswells are by now installed worldwide. They are not commonplace; the company is still new and struggling, but it has acquired that special momentum associated with a well-conceived product that fills a huge and hungry need. The machine has succeeded primarily in the business community and in countries where English is not spoken. But it will probably be a very long time indeed before the Boswell or anything remotely like it is made available for the serious, intensive instruction of children in the United States. Perhaps it works just a little too well.

It's relatively easy to install the Boswells in Russian schools, where the educational bureaucracy, like the whole country, is too exhausted and fragmented to notice or resist. Or in businesses, where there is a clear, immediate economic advantage to be gained by installing these astonishingly effective teaching machines. But in the U.S. public schools, it seems inevitable that the strongly rooted traditional educational system will protect itself against the advent of an electric teacher that costs, outright, a tiny fraction of the annual salary of its human equivalent.

The public schools have handled the emergence of computers as electric teachers in a characteristic way. Instead of resisting, they have sensibly dropped the whole problem into a neatly labeled box. The school allocates space for a formally designated "computer room." The room is filled with computer technology and placed under the control of a staff computer expert. The door is then quietly closed on this bright, modern-appearing technology ghetto.

By the turn of the century there will be as many computers in this country as there are people. Various estimates seem to converge at about 200 million computers now in place in businesses and homes. But in the school system, there are currently a paltry three million machines, or about one computer for every sixteen students. These computers are not easily integrated into the routine of the classroom, where they would obviously distract and divide the attention of the students and splinter the teachers' power to control the class. Computers are displayed to parents in the bright, modern computer room, but it is the parents' responsibility to guess that here is a technology under quarantine. And they do not guess it. It is a shame, because computers in public schools could have solved a major problem: teaching English to Americans.

The American Literacy Council estimates that there are twenty-seven million English-speaking but functionally illiterate adults in the United States. This is nearly 15 percent of the adult population: roughly one person in every seven cannot read or write well enough to understand a want ad or fill out a job application. This is not news. The blame for American ignorance of the English language has been sprayed in every direction. Illiteracy has been blamed on the schools, on social problems, on systems, on races, on values, on foreigners, on television, on politicians, and on children.

It is not widely understood, however, that the blame must fall first upon the English language itself. English is, as languages go, horribly designed.

In all English-speaking countries, illiteracy is widespread. England, India, Canada, and Australia, for example, share our difficulty in teaching people how to read and write English. Yet in other industrialized countries, the problem of functional illiteracy is not significant. Why not?

The reason is that most languages are spoken just as they are spelled. In Spanish, which is surely one of the most rational languages, there are just thirty-six sounds — and they are each faithfully represented by thirty-six unique letters or combinations of letters. Spanish is spelled exactly the way it sounds. If you can speak Spanish, you can easily read it and write it as well.

But the spelling of English words cannot be guessed or extracted from the sounds of English words. Here are some familiar examples: the characters *OUGH* signal to the reader five different sounds in the words *bough, cough, tough, through,* and *dough.* The last one, the long *O* sound, can be spelled in at least nineteen other ways. There are a few helpful rules ("I before E except after C," we chant), but the awful truth remains: learning to read and spell English requires massive, rote, boring, brute force memorization. The student must *eat* the English language, one word at a time.

So here is a clear-cut technical problem with a clear-cut technical solution. The problem is a language that must be learned by rote. The solution is a computer that has the infinite patience to teach it.

One other solution, incidentally, has long been urged, and that is to overhaul the English language. For hundreds of years, reform-minded Americans have undertaken campaigns to rationalize English spelling. Benjamin Franklin, Mark Twain, and Andrew Carnegie all had programs to fix English. Theodore Roosevelt tried to move the reform along by having all government publications printed using "phonic" spelling. He could not get this idea past Congress, although he is generally credited with having the word *gaol* reformed into *jail.*

After two centuries of futile attempts at spelling reform, it seems clear that it will never happen. This sounds like a trivial matter, perhaps even a joking matter, but bear in mind the human tragedies and the capital waste represented by that 15 percent of our population that is functionally illiterate.

Computers have been brought to bear on the problem with some success, notably in special remedial programs that are offered outside the daily routine of — and sometimes beyond the walls of — the public school systems. Such programs are provided in both the United States and Canada, for example, by government, civic, church, and business organizations. Their common quality is that they have small staffs and bitterly little money to work with. Teachers are often volunteers. Computers are welcome and eagerly received.

The American Literacy Council has developed and tested over a period of years the program Sound-Speler, which instantly corrects misspelled words like *speler* that sound intuitively right but aren't. The program recognizes common phonetic spellings and errors, and recognizes and corrects various American dialects. The key is in the instant feedback — the constant, endlessly patient correction of errors. Contrast the value of the computer's right-now response with, say, a graded exam paper returned to the student a week or so after the questions were asked.

Computers work. They deliver self-paced, one-on-one instruction. They are infinitely patient and quick to reward progress. Programmed intelligently, computers can be utterly engaging; the proof is in the power of video games. The teacher, in computerized instruction, is really the programmer. He or she is in effect cloned — multiplied — by the number of computers in use. Hence, for each student, a personal teacher.

There is more than just computer technology at issue here. There is a problem with a semantic error that is so deeply ingrained that it has become invisible. The problem is that the meanings of the paired, ethically loaded words *right* and *wrong* become hopelessly scrambled, in a conventional classroom, with the two ethically neutral terms *correct* and *incorrect*. As a result, students come away with the lesson that when they are wrong, they are *bad*.

The standard classroom repartee of teachers' questions and students' responses naturally rewards students who already know all the answers. Bright, cleanly scrubbed, middle-class students, who have been thoroughly preeducated by their parents, get plenty of strokes in school. They learn that they are right, and that they are good. The rest of the children, the "dumb" ones, the ones who are so often and so ludicrously wrong — they also learn a lesson: that they must keep their mouths shut in order to keep people from laughing at them.

There is nothing wrong with being wrong. We all learn through trial and error. But in a classroom, a teacher is also a judge of rightness, and the teacher's spoken or unspoken judgment ("you are wrong") is what many a student will carry into the world as a logical syllogism of human failure: I am wrong. Wrong is bad. Therefore I am bad. Over the years K through 12, this becomes an uncertain child's indelible lesson in self-esteem. That she is bad. That he is bad. That they are bad. Because they are wrong. These kids grow up to rob gas stations.

Computers never judge. They provide each student an infinite number of opportunities to learn. Mistakes are made, but they are made in private, in a secret dialog between the student and the machine. In other words, a computer does not absurdly punish the ignorant for their ignorance. It repeats. And repeats and repeats. It is never an embarrassment to the student to ask it to repeat just one more time. Nobody knows. Nobody sees. This is what the computer does differently. It takes the needless emotional punishment out of an education, and puts in its place the content of an education, which is simply knowledge.

If you wish to invest in computers in education, focus on companies that derive their income from educational software for use on computers installed at home, or in vocational training for businesses, or on specialized systems like the Boswell. And look overseas.

Companies selling to the U.S. school system must spend massively on lobbying that system. The growth in this field is an uphill slog, and the profitability history has been very discouraging. This is because the intended customers, the schools, do not really want the product. Companies that market internationally do better. Boswell International is a publicly traded company, although the stock is a highly volatile and speculative issue because the company is still very small. An Israeli company, Edusoft, based in Tel Aviv, traded on the NASDAQ, has done well with a range of software sold worldwide to educational institutions, vocational schools, and corporations.

Edusoft also enjoys some special tax incentives that typically accrue to Israeli-based technology companies. The tax break to the companies means, to their investors, that Israeli technology companies can profit earlier and better from their revenue dollars. This usually pays out as an accelerated rate of growth and, thus, a relatively faster gain on the stock market.

Edusoft forms partnerships with its larger customers, which have included Siemens, Berlitz, and Israel's Bank Leumi, among others. The cost of software development is either shared by or shifted to the partner. When the product is finished, Edusoft will typically return royalties to the partner. It thus sacrifices some profits on winners, but avoids a drain on capital while it waits to see if a product will work out. (Software products not uncommonly bog down in development, debugging, and beta-testing for long periods of time. Fee income really helps when product income is not yet coming in.) This business arrangement is similar in kind to the research partnerships often formed between large drug companies and biotechnology research boutiques.

For Siemens, Edusoft has created software to teach electronics to engineers and technicians. This is a subject that is a natural for teaching via computer, since animated illustrations (as of waveform diagrams) can be used to make circuitry make sense to the student very quickly. Concepts of timing and coincidence, which are central to understanding electronics, are much easier to display than to describe. The students can grasp these ideas most quickly from a computer screen. Electronics courses developed by Edusoft in partnership with Siemens are sold to other corporations. Siemens is rewarded for sponsorship of the programs' development with a royalty of up to 20 percent of the sales.

Altogether, Edusoft offers more than one hundred interactive, full-color educational software products in math, physics, biology, electronics, telecommunication technology, language teaching, and early childhood education. The library of instructional software is available in the major languages — some of the programs are available in fifteen different languages. This is because of the company's background, which has historically been in marketing to multilingual Europe. But it turns out to be helpful in marketing in the United States as well. An arithmetic teaching program that happens to be available in both English and Spanish is an especially attractive product in south Texas, Miami, and California.

Edusoft software, which is marketed in the United States from their Orlando office as Edustar software, is presented here as an example of what to look for in selecting stocks of companies working this field. It is not dependent on sales to U.S. school systems. It has substantial international and corporate markets. And the company does business in such a way as to cut back on the capital risks associated with new product development. These are all positives.

The corporate and home markets for educational software are especially important. The peculiar problems inherent in public educational systems have never been solved, and there is no reason to imagine they can be solved. The schools will probably continue to successfully deflect the concept of computerized education, so don't invest in it. Computers that teach are finding their real markets in home instruction and in reeducation, that is, using computers to quickly convey remedial adult language and vocational skills.

Businesses can help. Whole generations of computers are regularly superseded and replaced. We need some mechanism to enable the donation of these machines directly to individual students, as a sort of electronic Big Sister/Big Brother program. It is not an adequate solution to donate machines to schools and take the writeoff. To *really* do the job, each computer should be packed with software and delivered directly to a child's home.

Chapter 15

Imaging as Work

IN THE WRITINGS OF FUTURE economic historians, it will probably be remarked that in the late twentieth century, a major economic and technical upshift occurred, as follows: human labor was invested less and less in adding value to tangible objects and more and more in adding value to images.

The computerized image business now includes the computer-aided design of manufactured parts and of buildings; the graphic arts; desktop publishing; aerial and geophysical mapping; medical diagnostic imaging and image enhancement; video games; color and page processing; and machine vision. The power of computers to manipulate images on a screen (to preview printed photos, 2-D and 3-D engineering drawings, blueprints, and pages) has been used to advantage in publishing, graphics, architectural design, and engineering for many years. Within the past decade, new businesses have grown in this field, declined into obsolescence, made comebacks. Imaging continues to be a volatile and suddenly shifting technology.

Computer imaging is especially promising, just now, because computers have finally arrived at a practical power to recognize and understand the images they "see" and display. I first saw this new pattern recognition capability at work in a serology laboratory in Davis,

California. The blood typing laboratory is a facility of the veterinary school of the University of California. The lab has a contract with the American Jockey Club to run blood tests to verify the paternity of racehorses.

It is a bigger business than one might imagine. The lab processes 72,000 samples of horse blood per day. To test one horse, each of 142 separate blood-test reactions must be examined under a microscope to determine whether the blood has clotted. For a human lab technician, this is an easy call. The blood looks clumpy or not. But no human wants to examine 72,000 blood samples in a day. The problem is how to convey the concept of "clumpiness" to an uninstructed computer peering down the barrel of a microscope.

Wasyl Malyj (pronounced *molly*), chief development engineer at the serology lab, decided to try to teach a neural network system to spot and recognize clumped blood samples. Neural nets are computer programs that are capable of learning, as a human would, from trial and error. So Malyj fitted a video camera to a microscope, to give the computer a look at the subject matter. But consider his problem's magnitude.

This particular camera divides its field of view into 262,144 distinct pixels of visual information. In principle, it would be possible to feed this enormous array of data directly into the computer, but this would be a little like displaying all of human knowledge to a two-month-old baby. It is too much. To learn the concept of clumpiness, the computer could be shown tens of thousands of microscope slides, but Malyj estimated that the time required for his computer to get the idea, through repeated trials and errors, would have been on the order of twenty-eight million years.

This is not a special problem. It illustrates the enormous difficulty associated with giving computers the power of sight. It hints at why companies that pioneered this technology in the 1970s and 1980s were, as a group, dismal investments. So Wasyl Malyj, an engineer working in the relative obscurity of the vet school serology lab in Davis, California, in a steel outbuilding surrounded by pleasant pastures and stables, was attempting to solve a problem that had frustrated an industry. To make the network function in the here and now, Malyj knew he had to discover a shortcut.

He found it in a long-neglected scientific paper originally published in 1970 by George Lendaris, an expert in scanning aerial surveillance photographs by computer. Lendaris, who did this work at a

General Motors military research laboratory in Santa Barbara, was also coaxing his computer to simulate the human eye. The object was to ferret out from aerial photographs any orderly or repetitive patterns on the ground: orchards, road intersections, buildings, and rows of buildings are examples. Another is an array of military equipment, such as emplaced artillery.

Lendaris's computers had encountered the same problem as Malyj's. They could not digest the photographic images whole. Too much data. But Lendaris found he could massively reduce the amount of raw information that had to be processed by first running a commonplace mathematical algorithm called the Fourier transform. The effect is to ignore most of the trivial background data in the picture, and to selectively pluck out repeating features and sharp gradations like, say, the edges of buildings or the lines of gun barrels.

In Malyj's application, the transform can help pick out the edges of a clump of blood. The technique hugely simplified the problem. Aided by the Fourier transform, Malyj found that he could condense the 262,144 pixels from a single microscope slide into a mere forty-eight data points. His neural net computer was quickly able to learn how to determine, from the forty-eight features, whether a clump of blood is present. What had long been impossible for conventional computing logic became possible using a neural network.

As computers acquire the gift of sight, the neat industry categories still commonly used to classify the image-based businesses, as investments, have begun to blur and break down. This technology has outstripped its original goals and early limitations. Visual images processed by computer have become an important growth industry.

Most of the new companies are using commonplace computers, along with specialized hardware and software, to improve our view — pushing out the frontiers of this late-twentieth-century phenomenon of computerized image creation, display, manipulation, and pattern recognition. Nobody really knows exactly how to define this field, or quite where the edges are. It is obvious from their earnings, however, that imaging companies can pay their own way and then some.

The profit margins are excellent, but as an investor you must pick and choose, and understand clearly that what's hot today may be swept aside in a year or so by emerging competitors or even higher technologies. Here are sketches of four companies whose stocks are representative of the type.

Computers that can see have a pivotal role to play in the future of manufacturing. They can locate objects, read labels and inscriptions, measure dimensions, and precisely position components for mounting or assembly. With this gift of sight, manufacturing machines can often work faster than fingers, and can deal with objects too small to see well with the naked eye or too massive to precisely position by hand. Cognex, of Boston, is still small but is the leader in this field. The company is pioneering Windows-based software to cut short the intricate programming normally required to adapt machine vision to customers' manufacturing processes.

Electronics for Imaging of San Mateo, California, was formed in 1989 by technology superstar Efi Arazi, who revolutionized (and then dominated) the technology of color separations for printing with the laser scanning equipment of his previous venture, Scitex. This time, the product is a hardware/software package for desktop publishers who are equipped with high-speed digital printers. The EFII system makes it possible to print *short* runs of high-quality full-color publicity pieces, and thus enables its customers to capture an attractive segment of the traditional commercial printers' market or, for corporate graphics departments, to bring this type of business in-house. Copy centers are major customers. The technology will completely change the economics of brochures, cut deeply into the business of the printing industry, and enable sellers to tailor product publicity to pique the interests of specific demographic groups of customers.

Corel Corporation of Ottawa, Ontario, sells a highly regarded and successful software package called Corel Draw. It integrates in one package all the major graphics functions: illustration, charting, photo editing and painting, animation, and presentation graphics. Here is the type of "hard" specialized software that builds a substantial following over time, because it must be learned, and the benefits of this are such that an analyst has characterized Corel's position in graphics software as "a stronghold." The stock is traded on both the NASDAQ and Toronto exchanges.

In engineering and architectural design, computer-aided-design (CAD) software is now commonplace, but there are trends in this technology that investors can recognize and play. One is the gradual downward migration of engineering design work from mainframes to minicomputers to workstations to desktop computers. A leader in workstation CAD software is Parametric Technology. Parametric software does more than draw pictures of machines: it maintains an intelligent awareness of designs in progress.

In practice, let's suppose an engineer has specified some standard-sized bolt and nut for application throughout the construction of, say, a structural steel truss. Subsequently he decided to upgrade to a slightly larger nut-and-bolt standard. In a "dumb" CAD system, he would be required to meticulously redraw and specify every bolt hole in the truss. But with Parametric's software, the system knows enough about the project to change the dimensions of all the holes automatically.

The distinction between workstations and PCs is going to vanish in the course of the next few years. This will create a wider market for software of this type, simply by making it less expensive to purchase computer systems that can run it. CAD software, like publishing software, is designed to do a special job. It is used by specialists and is therefore blessed with some inherent price protection. A so-called vertical or specialized software product like Parametric Technology's is not immune to price competition, but it will never become a commodity product. It builds a loyal following among its users, and for this reason such stocks have good medium-to-long-term prospects.

Chapter 16

The Internet Juggernaut

W HEN THE INTERNET suddenly became a household word in the mid-1990s, it seemed to many people to have sprung up out of nowhere. In the spring of 1995, a study reported that more than 20 million cyberspace enthusiasts worldwide were already hooked into the Internet. The news was greeted with astonishment. Suddenly there existed a huge new city on this planet, and it was bigger than New York, bigger than Tokyo. It was a city without a country: bound by no country's law, impeded by no country's borders or tariffs. But precisely where were the *stores* in this city? In other words: Shouldn't there be some way to turn this new mass phenomenon, the Internet, into a mass market?

The Internet was conceived in the late 1960s, when its prototype, which was called the ARPAnet, was set up by the U.S. Department of Defense. The idea was to establish a defense and research computer network that could survive massive bombing. Each node in the net stood alone but communicated readily with every other node by means of a standard communication protocol called the Internet Protocol. Phone lines, wires, and switching systems could be bombed out of the system, yet the computers could still communicate via whatever links survived. The protocol became an accepted standard for linking computers and networks of all kinds.

Over time, with the proliferation of small computers and small networks, the system has evolved into the Internet, a global electronic marketplace for ideas and information. Because this information is stored in such diffuse fashion on the Internet, written upon the disk drives of an astronomical number of individual computers, the system has come to resemble in certain ways a working model of a human brain. But it is a collective brain, shared by millions. An American in Omaha might muse over a catalog published on the Internet by a garden tool supplier in New Zealand. A Finn might correspond via electronic mail with a Nordic skiing enthusiast in Colorado. A woman in Manhattan might discover in China a folk remedy for her allergy to cats.

When skeptics questioned the accuracy of the new city's 20 million population figure, many in the business community were frankly relieved. The Internet looked like an opportunity, but it also looked like customers going somewhere else, into cyberspace, wherever that might be. But if the Internet population count was optimistic at 20 million in the mid-1990s, this was no reason to write off the Net as a passing fancy. This number would soon seem too conservative by half. The Internet was growing and drawing strength like a great gathering worldwide storm.

It was not really new. Viewed as a social phenomenon, the Internet had been forthcoming for a decade by 1995, for it represented the logical culmination of a relentless computer network interconnection movement that had been surging since 1985. The appearance of the Internet was an inevitable fusion step that all networks undergo as they mature. In this book they have been generically characterized as supernets. For example, in the final decade of the nineteenth century, the independent railways of Britain fused to create a nationwide railway network, that is, a supernet. The early proprietary railways, which were already extensive in their own geographic domains, were finally interconnected. Thanks to the new links, the public was given an exciting new awareness that the rails suddenly "went everywhere." Telephone, airway, roadway, and television networks mature in the same way — apparently overnight — through the fusion of already existing networks. So too with computer networks.

The railways began to fail as businesses when their formerly proprietary networks fused into a great national public utility, a common carrier. They lost monopoly privileges and profits because they out-grew the essential geometry of a monopoly — the hub and spokes. When networks are overlaid and fuse to form a Cartesian grid, the new huge network is not likely to make extraordinary profits for any one company. Instead, it helps create reasonable profits for every company. In this important commercial sense the Internet resembles the interstate highway network. Nobody owns it, everybody benefits from it. Allusions to the Internet as a public information superhigh-way are not so silly after all.

To proceed as an investor in Internet stocks, it is essential to un-derstand as a first principle that the Internet has no hub, no center.

We know, for example, that Microsoft controlled the personal computer business and enjoyed net margins near 25 cents on the dol-lar, year after year, because it controlled, from the beginning, the cen-ter of each computer. The hub of every IBM-compatible PC is its central processor chip, and the traffic in and out of this hub is con-trolled by a Microsoft standard operating system. It is urged, absurdly, that some company — perhaps Microsoft, perhaps Netscape, per-haps Sun Microsystems — will now seize the center of the Internet. This is absurd because the Internet has no center to seize.

Nobody will seize control of the Internet and turn it into a colossal profit machine like, say, the Bell Telephone network of bygone years. The Internet is not new, and so there is no question of training its growth like that of a young plant. The Internet is old — a vast and al-ready fully fused public utility. It is all spokes, and it has no hub. It cannot be monopolized.

How, then, do we account for the astounding stock market success of the prototypical Internet stock, Netscape? Netscape's product is a computer program called the Netscape Navigator. It is a web browser, that is, a tool that enables users to explore the content of the Internet's World Wide Web. Netscape has as yet achieved no monopoly. It is succeeding in the same way Compaq succeeded. It is a monopoly breaker.

When Netscape Communications, of Mountain View, California, came public in August 1995, it was a one-year-old company with scant revenues and no earnings. The press reveled in the news that the com-pany's founder was a twenty-four-year-old computer wizard, Marc Andreesson, who is now senior vice president of technology for the public company. (These same accounts rather deemphasized the role of the new company's chairman, Jim Clark, a seasoned entrepreneur whose track record of previous successes included the creation of Silicon Graphics.)

The price of the stock on its initial day of offering oscillated wildly between $27 and $37, split adjusted, but at the end of the trading day, the company had acquired a market value of $2 billion. There ensued a predictable spate of newspaper articles tut-tutting about technology stocks in general. I tore one of these essays out of a daily newspaper and underlined all of the following words: *mania, frenzy, hype, froth, craze, crash,* and *hysteria*. The piece even included the pat recitation of the cautionary tale from the *The Madness of Crowd*s about the manic speculation in tulip bulbs in the seventeenth century. I began to take an interest in Netscape.

As is the case with most initial public offerings, the stock went into reverse soon after the opening day, and it bottomed on August 30, 1995, near $23. It then began a remarkable upward spiral. On December 6, it hit a high of $87. It appeared that the stock kept ratcheting higher as short sellers — sensing a sure thing — sold into this obviously irrational, idealistic, ridiculous rally. The short sellers lost a lot of money very quickly, and were subsequently forced to buy their way out of their predicament. Their panic buying pushed Netscape's stock higher still.

The rally affected all the stocks that represented plays on the growth of the Internet, including perhaps most notably UUnet Technologies and Spyglass. UUnet was the Internet service provider to Microsoft; and Spyglass was a rival to Netscape in the browser business. Both stocks tripled their original offering prices in the course of the year.

Morgan Stanley made it possible to trade a basket of securities of companies with a stake in the future of the Internet — comprising an Internet index. When the bubble finally popped, in December, the Internet stocks went into headlong retreat. Significantly, Netscape proved resilient. It fell from $87 to $35, and then doubled to $72 in just two months. A trader of my acquaintance remarked of Netscape that "this [approximately] gosh-darned stock is a pogo stick," while other Internet stocks languished.

At year end, Netscape reported a loss of $3.4 million, but significant revenues of $81 million. By May 1996, the company had secured a dominant share of market for network browser software — 85 percent of the market despite the appearance of many rival products. The company had also woven a network of its own, forming important strategic alliances with major on-line services and hardware and software manufacturers, including Hewlett-Packard, Apple, and Oracle.

Netscape was essentially giving away its products to consumers. If you had access to the Internet, you could freely download beta test copies of the latest Netscape Navigator, or free copies of obsolescent versions of the program. Not only was this stuff free, it was terrific. Users were encouraged to look to Netscape as the leader and standard setter in Internet technology — as indeed it was. The similarity to Compaq again comes to mind. Netscape, like Compaq, was using its substantial front-end capital to buy and lock up a huge early share of market.

Meantime, Netscape was also beginning to make quite a lot of money selling software into corporate environments. This other market, which is sometimes called the "Intranet," was pioneered by Net-Manage of Cupertino, California, in the early 1990s, before the Internet caught fire with the general public. NetManage wrote software that adapted the free-flowing computer communications technology of the Internet to networks operating within the walls of corporations. The NetManage product line consisted of forty-two programs that accomplished basic tasks like transferring files between dissimilar computers or linking a Windows computer to a minicomputer running the UNIX operating system. NetManage's vice president told me the company had first tried to locate a consumer market for Internet software, but quickly concluded that "the Internet is where the money isn't." At that early point in time, this was true.

NetManage then turned to corporations developing internal networks, an intramural market they dubbed the Intranet. This worked. In 1994, NetManage's revenue tripled to $62 million, and it was identified by *Fortune* as the fastest-growing software company in America. NetManage was reaching into a corporate communications market originally identified by Lotus Development; Lotus succeeded in it with its Lotus Notes software. But NetManage's approach had significant cost advantages. IBM bought out Lotus Development with an interested eye on the Lotus Notes business, but that business was already drifting to companies like NetManage and then — ultimately and significantly — to Netscape.

NetManage's growth rate slowed in late 1995, and the stock stumbled badly in early 1996. There seems little question that its new rival, Netscape, with its extremely high visibility, familiar user interface, and important strategic alliances with major hardware manufacturers, was making strong competitive inroads into the Intranet market. Netscape had become a commercial force to be reckoned with, not merely a stock market wunderkind.

Yet in the early summer of 1996, a *Barron's* survey of portfolio managers determined that Netscape and one other Internet stock were the two *least* popular stocks, among portfolio managers, of all the fifteen thousand stocks on the stock market. For a contrarian investor, it would be difficult to imagine a stronger hint that the time had come to buy Netscape's shares.

One can only speculate about why Netscape, which appeared to be doing everything right, would become so unpopular in the financial community. Two reasons suggest themselves: The portfolio managers (1) lost money on the stock by going short or selling calls and/or (2) did not make money on the stock, that is, failed to participate in its prodigious runups. Clients asked of these managers: "Where were you on the day Netscape went public?" The only answer to this question was, of course, harumph.

If Netscape is breaking a monopoly, then precisely whose monopoly is it breaking? Business writers, who understand very well that the best stories are based on the drama of a conflict, have declared a direct rivalry between Microsoft and Netscape. It makes good copy. In these stories Microsoft is portrayed as a stiffening but still grasping and dangerous monopoly, and Netscape is the upstart challenger. There are a few elements of truth in this scenario, but the monopoly under challenge is only rather incidentally Microsoft's, and the challenger is not Netscape. The monopoly is that of the established media, and the challenger is the Internet. The Internet bypasses every other medium; it is the railroad suddenly discovered to be racing alongside the barge canals.

The barge canals?

All networked media, including the mediums of exchange, are at risk to the Internet, and will have to *change* in some way to profit by this new medium or lose out.

Television is obviously a barge canal. Print is another. Banking, and every other conventional medium for capital formation, including the stock markets, are others. All these media will eventually be subsumed within the Internet. Yes, you finally will be able to get 500 television channels one fine day. But they will probably arrive as latecomers, that is, 500 additional new channels, added as an increment to the 400,000 channels already available on the World Wide Web.

The list of subsumable media includes the telephone system, facsimile transmission, automobile and airline transport, and physical money.

These changes are out there in the blue sky of the twenty-first century, but the Internet frightens many businesspeople right now. This is why it is so roundly and commonly scoffed at, trivialized, logically boxed in, and written straight to the margins.

Much of *business* is really a medium. It exists to provide a conduit between an original source supplier (of goods or knowledge or capital) and an end user. A middleman is a *medium*. And it is the media, all media, that are most strongly challenged, affected, or threatened by the emergence of the Internet. This new medium, the Internet, cuts out the old middlemen, and presents a whole class of new middlemen — virtual retailers, virtual bankers and brokers, virtual educators, virtual doctors.

Over time this will obviously bring great dislocation and change to the civilization.

Here is a marketing paradox. Unlike television and newsprint, the Internet makes no attempt to appeal to everybody. Yet it appeals to each person far more strongly than any of the mass media. It is immensely frustrating to mass marketers that the Internet provides direct access to 20 million people — and yet cannot be made to conform to the accepted formula (that is, the TV formula) for selling products into a mass market. Although television cable is a superior transmission system for data, some marketing executives' fascination with distributing the Internet's services via a "set-top box" perched on a TV set is based on nostalgia — a wish that the Internet would behave like TV as a mass broadcasting medium. It never will.

The Internet cannot be used as a mass marketing medium for mass market products. Instead, the Internet appeals to each person individually, and sells products that appeal to very special interests. If you are a horse fancier, you can surround yourself with horse people, horse ideas, and horse-oriented products by tapping into the Internet. If you are a basket collector, you can find the most exotic and sophisticated basket suppliers on the Net. If you like nuclear physics, go to the Net. Ditto if you have a new baby in the house. If you suffer a particular chronic illness and want to compare notes with other sufferers, go to the Net. If you skydive, make love in a nonstandard way, or sell stepper motors — go to the Net.

Whatever you do, whatever you want, you can do it or get it better and faster with the help of the information available to you from like-minded people, worldwide, on the Internet.

The Internet will end the era of mass marketing aimed at the interests and tastes of median buyers. It will finally bring an end to the obsessive marketing analysis of Ozzie and Harriet, the prototypically median couple. The Internet makes it possible to market diverse products and services to diverse buyers. In the end, nobody will care any longer what the median purchaser wants. Every special interest will be piqued and served.

An on-line bookstore, Amazon.com, has already created a strong metaphor for this new kind of business specifically (and brilliantly) designed to serve diverse interests. In little more than a year on the Internet, Amazon.com has created a retail book business that outsells superstores. This business is built on *selectivity*. Browsers on the Internet can freely search for any book they are interested in. Not only can they run computer searches by author, subject, and title, as in a library — they can search using keywords. In five minutes on the Internet at the Amazon.com web site, a reader can immerse herself in listings and reviews of all the books available on any particular subject, from bareboat sailing to dog neuroses to you name it. A similar trek through a real bookstore could take hours. These would be pleasant hours, certainly, but a physical search is often frustrating. And no human could accomplish in a few hours such a comprehensive book search as that accomplished by Amazon.com's computers in a few microseconds.

How does Amazon.com differ, at root, from a traditional business? Instead of concentrating in one place a huge and diverse inventory of *objects* — books — Amazon.com simply concentrates and warehouses *information* about books. The business does not stock all the books it sells. When the orders come in, Amazon.com arranges for the delivery. The real product is a database of searchable information. The "store" is essentially a display case for this information, a virtual bookcase with the capacity (currently) for a million books.

This searchable bookcase is a fair metaphor for the Internet itself. Just now the shelves are filled with a zillion catalogs, mostly industrial and commercial catalogs. If you are a corporate purchasing manager, the Internet can be an indispensable tool. Because it is international, it is particularly helpful in expanding your lists of potential suppliers. If you have been buying mops by the gross in Brazil, maybe you could do a little better by buying them in Europe. Take a look. If you need to buy a supply of 4-40 hex nuts, analog semiconductors, cement trucks, pharmaceutical-grade chemicals, sofa stuffing — try the Net for comparative shopping. It is an established and accepted wholesale marketplace.

It is in retailing that the Internet has not yet thrived.

In the mid-1990s worldwide annual retail sales via the Internet amounted to only $324 million. Retailing was inhibited because few users were trusting enough to key their Visa or American Express numbers into a blank space provided on an Internet web site. Internet retailers had been trying to do business without a cash register, and it wasn't easy.

Netscape in mid-1996 unveiled a suite of new software products designed to make it much easier for retailers and their customers to actually do business on the Net. The umbrella name for these products is (unfortunately) LivePayment. It enables companies to accept credit cards with confidence, and consumers to use them with confidence. Neil Weintraut, an analyst who follows the Internet stocks for Hambrecht & Quist in San Francisco, promptly dubbed the new system with a far better name. He called it "the Buy Button."

Electronic commerce is complicated. Netscape is supplying and coordinating three elements: the sellers, the buyers, and the banks and financial institutions that enable credit card transactions. The Buy Button looks engagingly simple to the buyer, but it works because (1) the buyer has a particular software package, to wit, Netscape's Navigator, and (2) the seller has constructed a storefront, or web site, using Netscape software and (3) the banks recognize the legitimacy of the transaction and (4) web servers, computers that act as nodes in the Internet, are set up using Netscape software. Invisible threads that bind this system together are compatibility between the software of the seller and the buyer and — of supreme importance — encryption of the credit card numbers. From the outset, the system was supported by CyberCash, First Data Corporation, GE Capital Retailer Commercial Services, MasterCard, VeriFone, and Wells Fargo Bank.

The creation of a complex second network of protected commercial tunnels through the Internet can turn the wide acceptance of Netscape Communications software, over time, into a franchise of enormous value. As technology investors, this is exactly what we have learned to look for: a protected network.

There are a number of competing schemes to facilitate electronic commerce on the Internet, but at this stage, Netscape seems the most realistic and best-grounded investment in the Internet stock group. Bear in mind that Netscape's stock is indeed a pogo stick, and try to buy the dips. A dollar-cost-averaging program would be an appropriate way to build a position gradually over time.

A word to the wise. In the Internet stock sector there are some very flimsy companies with stocks on offer. Some promoters are obviously attempting to capitalize on naive investors' fascination with the Internet group, and I would be coldly cautious about investing in any of them.

Chapter 17

Biotech: That Painted Lady

THE BIOTECHNOLOGY STOCK GROUP has garnered the worst — the dirtiest — reputation of any stock group in the science-and-technology sector. The futuristic appeal of the science underlying this technology has been exploited by stock marketeers peddling worthless paper, and by scientists peddling their academic and research credentials to nominal "scientific advisory boards" intended to dignify the issue of worthless paper. Public excitement about medicines that promise miracles has been transformed into private fortunes made in stocks without products, revenues, earnings, or scientific legitimacy. Be it up or down, biotech is now widely understood to be the red-light district of the NASDAQ exchange.

The same paragraph could have been written about the railway mania in the English stock speculations of the nineteenth century, or about the incipient oil business in the twentieth. Biotechnology is the only major, transforming technology now in human prospect. It is in biotech that you should position, by the turn of the century, as much as 75 percent of capital earmarked for science-and-technology investments. It is a case of hold your nose and buy biotech.

The rules for protecting yourself are simple. First, look for those companies where revenue from products exceeds their revenue from fees and cash investments. Second, favor those companies whose medicines have already been granted approval for marketing by the Food and Drug Administration (FDA). Do not confuse an FDA approval with "a recommendation for approval." Formal approval is different, a real go-ahead to sell a product, and it may take years to be granted — even after the product has been recommended for approval by a committee of experts.

Investing folklore has it that in a given product cycle, half the runup in a biotechnology stock occurs after a formal approval is granted by the FDA. This seems a fair estimate to me. By waiting, you get half the run and none of the risk. If you bet on approval in advance, you may see double the runup of the more conservative investor — but to try for it you are taking a big risk.

Still, if you strictly follow the most conservative approach, you will probably not find more than four or five companies to invest in. The short list usually includes Genentech, Amgen, Chiron, Biogen, and Genzyme. This is in fact a good conservative core group for a biotech stock portfolio.

If you buy only the obvious five, however, you will automatically exclude some very good speculations.

Out of the 1,300-odd biotechnology companies, about a fifth, or 250, are public companies with stock you can buy. If you stipulate a market capitalization of at least $25 million, the list of candidate stocks drops to a manageable 100 possibilities.

Recall that market cap is the value the stock market puts on a given company. You can calculate it by multiplying the price of the stock by the number of shares outstanding. As an isolated number it is not too helpful, but when you compare it to the market caps of other biotech companies, in a ranking, you can determine what the market "thinks" of a given company relative to the other stocks in the biotech group. Such a ranking by market cap is published regularly by BioVenture Consultants of San Mateo, California, and is readily available by subscription.

Another cut you can make is based on the elimination of fraud, or at least the potential for fraud. Drugs typically are tested in clinical trials conducted overseas. Money — investors' money — may exit the country to conduct such tests, and it does not necessarily return to these shores.

The cost of overseas research and development (R&D) goes onto the financial statement as a legitimate expense. In most cases it is one. R&D is, after all, one of the most expensive things in the world. But be aware of the potential for abuses here. Texans sometimes smile over an oil patch gambit known as "the old dry-hole trick." Investors invest, a hole is *said* to be drilled in some remote foreign field, and guess what — no oil, darn it. No money left, either. Sorry, see you next time. Obviously the old dry-hole trick can be played in the biotech industry as well.

Other than money channeled out of the country, another thing to watch out for is the creation of pseudo-sales. This practice might surface in the form of a press release announcing a major contract awarded to some struggling biotech company by another company, which is usually (nominally anyway) a pharmaceutical manufacturer. If you don't instantly recognize the names of the companies, check around a little. Sometimes it turns out that the two companies have a lot in common — such as the same owner. This is not a good sign at all. Try to sidestep these most obvious types of stock scams.

How to narrow it down from this point? Quantitative techniques are not too helpful because most of these companies have no beans to count. No products, no sales, no profits. The money they require to continue operating comes in from venture capitalist groups, from investment bankers, and from issuance of additional shares. The biotechnology industry runs through about $6 billion per year. The money comes from financial sources or, very significantly, from the formation of partnerships or collaborative arrangements with the major pharmaceutical companies.

Biotech companies that are public and without products must regularly report the rate at which they consume money, in the form of quarterly losses. In the near vacuum of quantitative information about biotechnology companies, number-starved analysts have seized upon these few available data points and used them to construct indexes with deeply ominous names: the burn rate index, for example, or the survival index. If you know how much cash a company has raised, and the rate at which it is burning through that money (the cash burn rate), it is possible to fix a precise date in the future when that company will run out of money completely.

I think these calculations are made simply because they *can* be made, and reported because they are inherently scary numbers. They have the same appeal to journalists as calculations showing precisely when the earth just might collide with an incoming comet. Viewed in isolation, the cash burn rates don't really inform investors, because they don't help us guess which companies will be able to refuel their cash tanks before supplies run out. The ability to gain new cash depends on qualitative factors. Good contacts, good selling, good science.

The method biotech startups must use to get their money from venture capitalists and investment bankers does suggest that the purchase of a biotech company as a new issue should be completely avoided. Wait until the stock has been on the market for two years. The original investors view the issue of stock to the public as the opening ("At last," they utter, "oh, thank God") of an exit path for themselves. Selling their very cheaply purchased shares to the public is the way they get rich, basically, so it is well to wait until after they have taken their profits and gone on. So here is another helpful way to carve down your risk — eliminate from consideration any biotech companies that have been public for less than two years.

Some additional ideas on how to select from the more speculative stocks are provided in the next chapter. In general, the idea is to pick "method" companies, that is, companies betting on techniques rather than on specific products. To see why this helps, let's first ask why the industry has acquired its gaudy reputation.

The biotech group proceeds from crash to crash. Consider that it has now been a decade and a half since the biotechnology industry first began to emerge as publicly held companies. Many of them did not hesitate to raise investors' expectations by hyping drugs that were years away from the market. The sad lesson for these companies and their shareholders is that there can be a very long wait between a press release and a product release.

Over the span of the 1980s, only seven distinct and highly significant products were brought to realization by the fledgling industry. Commercial biotechnology has such a tiny factual history that it can be told in detail in three paragraphs, which follow. (The history of biotech hype would of course fill volumes.)

The first three products were launched by Genentech between 1982 and 1986: insulin, which it licensed to Eli Lilly; human growth hormone, which Genentech kept; and an immune system stimulator, alpha interferon, which was licensed to Hoffmann-LaRoche. (An alpha interferon was also developed at Biogen and licensed to Schering-Plough.)

In 1986, Chiron's hepatitis-B vaccine came on the market. Merck makes it under license. In the same year, Johnson & Johnson's Ortho Pharmaceuticals introduced OKT-3, a drug that helps prevent kidney transplant rejection. In 1987, Genentech brought out its tissue plasminogen activator (TPA, trademarked as Activase), which dissolves blood clots, notably in heart attack patients. Finally, in 1989, Amgen began selling its Epogen brand of erythropoietin, an antianemia drug. In the aggregate, worldwide sales of these seven major products generated just $1.25 billion annually at the end of the decade. Not much of an industry. Yet in the following year, 1990, $2 billion was raised in stock market offerings for biotech companies, or about $750 million more than the industry's product sales.

Why? The reason was Amgen, a vigorous little company in Thousand Oaks, California. This stock came from nowhere in particular, a long summer doldrum near $9 — but in just two years it cracked $90 on the basis of real revenue and earnings growth for erythropoietin. We gained more than 600 percent on an early recommendation of Amgen.

This company and its product showed a skeptical stock market what biotechnology was capable of. Suddenly, the stock market couldn't get enough of biotech. The phrase "another Amgen" supplanted "another Xerox" in the routine sales palaver of retail stock brokers.

Speculative fever was fanned by the introduction of new products in the first two years of the 1990s. In fact, as many biotech products were introduced in these two years as had been issued in the entire preceding decade. The stock market bubble ultimately burst. Fortunes were duly lost. Reputations were lost. And innocence, if any, was also lost. Consider the price trajectory of Centocor stock, a piece of paper that changed in value from $6.63 to $60 and back to $6 in less than five years. Synergen, on news of its failure to obtain FDA approval for a new product, dropped from $41 to $13 in a single day. Many investors are so disgusted with biotech that they will never buy another share of it. So there is value to be found in biotech now, a discount associated with even the better biotechs — a discount from disgust and mistrust.

I did my graduate work in biochemistry, and it once seemed reasonable to me that science should provide some sort of a solid peg for sorting out the values of these stocks. For a *Forbes* column, I arranged a cooperative study with the publishers of the *Science Citation Index* in Philadelphia. The *Science Citation Index* is a statistical compendium of the number of citations received by a given scientific paper in other, subsequently published scientific papers. The index helps quickly identify scientific work that is attracting the attention of scientists. Such data are typically used, for better or worse, to determine the visibility and standing of research institutions, universities, and individual scientists. But what interested me was the relative ranking, scientifically, of the publicly held companies in biotechnology.

The results were surprising. In a top ten ranking, the companies with the best (or anyway, the most remarked) science were Chiron and Genentech. These are also successful businesses, so at the zenith of the list virtue is indeed rewarded. But for companies ranked 3 through 10, the correlation flipped completely. The company with the least remarked science was Amgen — which was far and away the best business. The correlation between good science and good revenues, in other words, is inverse.

It is a puzzle, but makes sense in the end, and in a way that signals profound changes in the way this science is pursued. If you publish your ideas, you are handing them away to the competition. If you keep your ideas to yourself, you are gaining ground commercially. Academic achievement is closely tied to publication volume, but it seems clear that in the future, biotechnology will progress in the secrecy of private laboratory settings. Commerce rewards secrecy.

It is an unusual case. When you invest in semiconductor technologies, it is indeed a technology — an applied science — that you are buying. When you invest in biotech, you are often buying pure science, a science that stands on the shoulders of academic research of many decades past. But it will probably move up from here in private. This is widely resented, for private companies are now clearly benefiting from years of public investment in biochemical research. But it is the case.

We are living, according to the American Association for the Advancement of Science, in the golden age of biology. Molecular biology has been to the second half of this century what nuclear physics was to the first. But the payout — the profits from the technology grounded on the spectacular progress of a single science — has begun only in the past few years.

Biotechnology is golden because it never has to wholly invent products. The products — or at least the templates against which products can be constructed — already exist. The technology consists of various tricks that can be used to pull off the shelf already finished and tested products — molecules that are known to have certain chemical activities in nature. More tricks can be used to fabricate their obverse or mirror images. The basic products are fantastically efficient protein molecules already fully developed and finely elaborated by nature — by evolution — over the span of the past four billion years.

Nature has done the basic R&D — has been working at it for eons. All we have done in this field so far is to thumb open a product brochure here and there. You can safely regard all the recent products — successes and failures alike — as a mere tiny sampler from an immense natural catalog.

Long before the investment capital influx of the early 1990s, and over a period of many decades, investment has been loaded into biotech from the government, the foundations, private funding sources, and the pharmaceutical industry. It is this long-term investment by the society that enables little biotech companies to so vigorously launch themselves into the market. Gradually, over two generations, we have cocked a catapult.

The payout in biotech was slow in coming. It has taken us since 1952 to finally see substantial profits from commercial biotechnology. In these forty-odd years, much simpler technologies (semiconductors, notably) have bloomed, boomed, lost their novelty, and turned into commodities. Biotechnology, because it is so deeply complicated, has only now begun to make its run. The volatility in these stocks is astounding. Some are obviously scams, some are innocent blunderers — a few are good businesses. But the idea that biotechnology is a mere overnight success or purely speculative bubble is completely absurd. On the basis of the energy, intelligence, and capital invested over four decades in this group, the biotechs have a very long and fruitful payout period ahead of them.

Biotechnology companies have always been held out by their underwriters as distinct from pharmaceutical companies. The early, technical distinction was that the biotech companies used drug factories that were alive — cells — but pharmaceutical companies can now easily accomplish the same thing. The differences between the two groups seem to undergo constant redefinition. Depending on how you define this difference, you can declare that it has narrowed or widened over the years, or that it has vanished, or that it is irreconcilable. My personal favorite distinction between the pharmaceuticals and the biotechs is that they have followed two different paths toward the same hopelessly obsessive goal. This goal is the creation and protection of "blockbuster" drugs.

Blockbusters are drugs for which a mass market exists. A reasonable threshold level might be a drug producing gross annual sales ranging upward from $300 million. Historically, the billion-dollar blockbusters have been drugs that alleviate anxiety (Valium is the prototype, Prozac is the latest) and ulcers (Tagamet, Zantac). Notice first that these drugs are treatments, not cures. Most drugs that produce a very specific cure do not have a strong long-term market. Such a drug gets repeat business — if it is an antibiotic, for example — but it does not become part of a patient population's daily, open-ended regimen. Insulin does. Insulin is the prototype of a blockbuster drug.

Accordingly, if you are a drug researcher looking for a blockbuster, you must focus on providing limited-term relief for a chronic condition. Insulin, a drug for diabetes, is a good business because of the requirement for repeated administration over time in the management of the disease. The ulcer medicines were blockbusters because ulcers don't go away. (Or didn't, until it was determined that ulcers arise from an infection and that the infection is curable through antibiotics. To a marketer of treatments, there can be no worse business news than the discovery of a cure.)

You cannot know these things about the pharmaceutical business without acquiring a certain grim line in your mouth when the subject of blockbuster drugs comes up. Yet it is logically difficult to understand why the industry's fixation on creating mass-market treatments should strike us as a bad thing. Drug companies are in business to make money; it is what they do. They would rather make treatments than cures because treatments are better business. This does not mean they ignore or suppress cures — they actively look for them, of course. As an investor, you should also be alert to the limited business appeal of cures. A broker who wishes to sell you a stock in a company "with the cure for" (fill in the blank) is not putting you on the right track for the long term.

We as a society help support biological research seeking cures. This is because it is in the common interest, and because cures are a poor prospect for selfish interests. The society helps bankroll the search for cures because there is no great profit in them for the drug industry.

The major drug companies have been built on blockbusters. Just a few drugs, a mere handful of pills really, have created the great drug companies. Blockbuster drugs are treatments. When a single block-buster drug goes off patent, the loss of protected revenues can cripple and even destroy a major pharmaceutical company.

Let's say biomedical research in the United States costs $20-plus billion annually. Half is funded by the government, the other half by the industry — that is, by the pharmaceutical industry and the biotechnology industry. But while pharmaceutical companies plow back into research a percentage of the revenues from their products, the biotech companies are, for the most part, without products. They are plunging their front-end capital into research. Little wonder the biotechs are captivated by the business formula that worked so well for the pharmaceutical companies and for Amgen. Most of them are searching — some of them desperately — for blockbusters of their own.

The blockbuster obsession has led directly to most of the major stock market debacles in biotech. The story is always the same. A biotech company has come up with a treatment for a chronic or wide-spread disease. The market is estimated to be at least $300 million an-nually. The FDA has an approval right on the tip of its tongue. The approval has been fast-tracked. The approval is imminent. The ap-proval has been formally recommended by the advisory committee. A thousand brokers breathe the word *approval* over a thousand phones, it becomes a nationwide benediction, a stock market mantra. The stock scrapes the ceiling, breaks through the ceiling, flies straight up to Mars.

Approval is withheld by the FDA.

Next morning headlines in the business pages report that the stock has lost 33 percent of its value. Sometimes it is worse. Sometimes it is 50 percent or 75 percent or more.

Within days, the company's senior management is ousted for hav-ing risked so much to achieve so little. Nothing, in fact. Class action suits are filed in rapid-fire fashion on behalf of shareholders, who are said to have been misled. The stock rallies a notch — a last rally — as short sellers buy the stock in order to take their profits. The stock may never recover. And in the end, here is the result: no blockbuster.

As an investor, there are a couple of quick signals that may help you step to one side of these stock cycles, or to play them with options. First, examine the company's press releases. (A secondary industry has grown around the issuance of biotechnology press releases. They are free and plentiful.) Watch for the specific number, $300 million. This number is virtually a warm-up cliché, like the phrase "ladies and gentlemen." When you hear or see news of a $300 million market, you should be able to guess the rest of the story. More obvious danger signals are the familiar words *chronic* and *treatment*.

The inherent strength of biotechnology is not in its power to turn up blockbusters. It is in its power to field lots of different drugs with diverse biological effects.

To see where this leads, ultimately, consider that a hundred years from now, unique medicines will probably be created on the spot in the physician's office, custom tailored by automated synthesizers, for your specific body and your specific disease. Diseases that avoid destruction by changing their identity, like malaria and AIDS, could conceivably be defeated by rapid-fire custom drug synthesizers. In such a way the medicine could be made to keep ahead of the bug.

But there is no place for a concept like this in the current marketplace. Drugs are created and tested in massive clinical trials for mass consumption by the mass markets. The FDA approval cycle requires mass standardization. It is the ethic of the Model T Ford. It leads to mass production of a rigorously standardized product. Customized production would be very much against the law, and also against the grain.

Yet the real strength of biotechnology is not mass production at all, but diverse production of diverse molecules for diverse markets. To see how well this capability can work, consider Genzyme.

Genzyme is a Boston company whose management seems to have always understood that blockbusters sing a siren song. The president, Henri Termeer, instead focused his resources on capturing small monopolies in niche drug markets. A "small" drug is one that serves a small patient population — so small that if one company can capture a large share of its market, it becomes uneconomical for any competitor to bother contesting the rest. Genzyme built for itself a portfolio of such drugs, collecting tiny monopolies like stamps, until it finally assembled a quite large and largely impregnable monopoly.

Genzyme's market capitalization is now nearing $1 billion, which puts it fifth or sixth from the top of the industry — but while it was building its business, few analysts found it remotely interesting. As recently as 1989, it was widely regarded in the financial analytical community as a small-bore, an also-ran. I think Genzyme is an important case study because of Termeer's constant, steady emphasis, over a period of many years, on multiple diverse products. With this strategy, Genzyme played to the real inherent strength of biotechnology, which is its power to produce variety — not blockbusters.

If we leave to one side the distinction between mass production and diverse production, there is another difference in the relative strengths of biotechnology companies and pharmaceutical companies. Pharmaceutical companies have developed and maintained sales and marketing networks over the years, and the relatively tiny biotech companies have no sales networks in place. This is one reason the biotech boutiques have typically formed alliances and collaborative agreements with the major pharmaceutical companies — to see their products sold via the pharmaceutical company sales networks.

The absence of proprietary marketing networks — and the high cost of developing such a network de novo — has long been regarded as a major weakness of the biotech industry. Recently, however, this situation flipped. Major pharmaceutical houses may see their sales networks made superfluous by health-care reform legislation that shifts the decision to purchase specific drugs into the hands of relatively few key professional buyers.

Unlike phone companies and electric utilities, the drug companies do not draw their commercial stamina from protected networks. Their first lines of defense against price competition are technology, patent protection, and high regulatory hurdles. The sales and marketing nets have been an outer line of defense and can be sacrificed, however painfully. Yet here is an area where a disadvantage of the biotech companies may evaporate. In this new regulatory environment, drug buyers' unions will apply price pressure to both the pharmaceutical and the biotech industries. But the downscaling and diminished importance of sales and marketing networks gives the biotech companies a somewhat more level playing field vis-à-vis the pharmaceutical companies.

Both the biotechnology and the major pharmaceutical manufacturers have another rival in the field of making medicines — the generic drug industry, which has enjoyed a vogue among stock speculators but is a poor choice for investors. The generic drug stocks skyrocketed on sharp profitability growth as several major blockbusters reached the end of their term of patent protection and "went generic." These successes must be understood as short-term phenomena that degrade quickly as the formerly proprietary drugs are transformed into commodities. Consider the price trajectory of

Marion Merrell Dow's branded drug Cardizem, a blockbuster anti-hypertensive. In early November 1992, on its last day as a patent-protected, branded product, a bottle of 100 Cardizem pills in 30-milligram doses sold at an average wholesale price of $39.19. Within two weeks after the drug went off patent, the wholesale price for the generic equivalent flashed down to $4 per bottle.

Generic drugs are cheap, and this has encouraged naive investors to view them as the future of the drug industry in an era of tight drug cost controls. They are not the future. Generic drugs are cheap because they are downloaded from the past. A drug that comes off patent has been price protected for seventeen years — but it was probably conceived over a quarter of a century ago. It is an old drug.

It is an historical accident that a number of blockbusters were conceived in the late 1960s and early 1970s — thus inflating the generic drug stock balloon of the early-to-mid-1990s. This pipeline from the past is not an inexhaustible source of future success. Evidently, ideas for new blockbusters dried up in the 1970s, so the incoming supply of important "new" generics will soon slow to a trickle.

Old blockbusters have an amazingly short run of profitability as generics (sometimes as short as two weeks), and after that they produce only marginal profits for the generic manufacturers. The supply of aging blockbusters coming off patent will dwindle in the late 1990s. To invest in the future rather than the past, it probably makes sense to overlook the generics and study instead the biotechnology group, with all its promise and all its problems.

Chapter 18

Biochemistry with a Method

IN TERMS OF BOTH CAPITAL STRENGTH and science, the strongest biotechnology company is actually a pharmaceutical company, Hoffmann-LaRoche — a very conservative, very Swiss, very expensive investment. Their Roche Holdings, Ltd., owns most of Genentech and is perhaps positioned to buy the rest. After that, Chiron, Biogen, Amgen, and Genzyme conclude the standard stock picker's list. This is too short a list, however, and so at this point it is necessary to consider how to take on more biotech risk, somehow, without building a bomb into your portfolio.

A rather too pat solution to this problem is to allocate a segment of your portfolio for the purchase of a biotechnology mutual fund. The assumption is that the mutual fund manager will be an expert or will be advised by experts, and that the fund will reduce your risk by spreading it across many different biotech stocks.

But you can probably do just as well or better by making your own picks. The five core stocks are obvious. You will need to add to this basket four or five more speculative stocks: longer shots. As for expert advice, you can get professional analytical help from a brokerage, but it is essential to use the right brokerage. In my opinion the best biotechnology analysts (well-informed realists, not cheerleaders) work at Hambrecht & Quist and at Alex Brown. Most of these analysts are trained as physicians or biochemists, and all of them are savvy about this business. It would be worth your while to open an account at one of these houses to gain access to their internally published research reports on biotechnology trends and companies. Another good source of news and expertise is BioVenture Consulting of San Mateo, which is staffed by biochemists and issues several timely, helpful, candid, and often iconoclastic industry publications, including a stock report.

To add some riskier companies to the portfolio without taking on really excessive risk, focus on companies that have themselves focused on *methods* for creating products, rather than on specific drugs. Two good examples of the type are Gilead Sciences and Agouron Pharmaceuticals. I am not recommending these specific stocks for your portfolio — although they are not bad picks. Rather, I am suggesting you use them as a model, a guide to what can work. The idea is that in biotechnology, where the risk is extreme, companies that own and emphasize methods above products risk less.

While investors are betting on their stocks, biotech labs are betting on molecules. Those companies with special methods for extracting or creating molecules have a diverse portfolio of molecules to try as drugs. If molecule A doesn't work, they can try B and then C. If all three are duds, the companies can cut their scientific losses and shift resources to another field. Because their core asset is a methodology, rather than any one specific product, the companies are less likely to run out of money. Their bigger brothers, the pharmaceutical companies, recognize the value of a methodology and will help out in a scrape.

Let's consider some of the problems associated with launching a new drug created by a company in the biotechnology industry. It is clear from a glance at the smallish number of such products that it is very, very hard to do. In the decade from 1982 to 1992, only 15 protein-based biotech products made it to the market. Since then, another 6 products have completed the gauntlet. Tested and awaiting approval by the FDA as of 1994 are 24 more products. Still in clinical trials are 295 additional products, but of these, only 49 are in phase III trials.

Phase III clinical trials are the last major hurdle to be crested before a company can ask the FDA for approval to take the product to market. From that point, approval supposedly takes an average of

eighteen months. But it can require much longer waiting periods —
many years, in some cases.

So here we are. The industry has put just 21 products on the market, and not all of these are commercially successful. From an investor's standpoint, perhaps the most interesting new products, at
least in the view of their own manufacturers, are those 49 drugs in
phase III trials, and the 24 awaiting approval.

Certainly a company with a product in phase III clinical trials is a
lower-risk bet than a company with no product, or a company with a
drug for which only laboratory tests have been completed. But when
a publicly held company moves its product ahead to phase III trials,
the company's stock price quickly rises to discount the promise implied by its drug's progress. It rises again when the trials are complete
and FDA approval is requested. But investors have seen biotech
stocks plummet again and again on news of their drugs' failures to receive FDA approval. To the companies and to their investors, a negative decision can be devastating.

Is something fundamentally wrong?

In the opinion of biochemist Cynthia Robbins-Roth, who is pub-
lisher of *BioVenture View,* part of the problem is that "proteins make
lousy drugs."

The difficulty is that protein molecules, like hamburgers, are readily digestible. They lose their medicinal activity in the process. The digestive process may occur in the stomach, where digestive enzymes
such as trypsin, chymotrypsin, and papain can snip protein chains into
little pieces. Further breakdown of protein drugs can occur in the
blood and in the cells. This is because the catabolism of protein is one
of the main things living organisms do.

To sidestep digestive enzymes in the stomach and intestine, most
of the biotechnology industry's current generation of products must
be injected rather than administered orally. This tends to restrict the
drugs' use to the treatment of acute illness in a hospital setting. Patients with chronic conditions requiring repeated doses would naturally prefer drugs that can be administered orally.

The biotechnology industry was founded on the promise of protein
drugs such as synthetic insulin, erythropoietin, and the interferons.
But as the limitations of proteins as drugs have become more evident,
these products are increasingly characterized as "first generation."

The problem does not really lie with proteins as drugs — they have enormous power. The problem is one of drug delivery. Proteins are complex, heavy, fragile, and rather floppy molecules that can cross biological barriers such as the skin or mucous membranes only with difficulty.

At the site of injection, at the moment of injection, the protein drug is highly concentrated. But by the time it reaches its site of action, where it can do some good, the drug may have been diluted, dissected, filtered, attacked, reshaped, mousebitten, partially denatured, and modified. Big, complicated proteins, notably monoclonal antibodies, may elicit an immune response from the patient. This means antibodies injected as medicine may themselves be attacked as invaders by the patient's own antibodies. This becomes a more serious problem on a second course of treatment. The patient's immune system will "remember" the medicine and quickly attack it.

If a protein drug could be packaged for transport through the blood, as for example in liposomes (tiny fatty capsules), then the drug might be delivered to the disease in higher concentrations and in better shape. But companies working in liposome technology have not yet had a dramatic success. It would be even better if proteins could be packaged for oral delivery. Alkermes, Inc., of Cambridge, Massachusetts, has reported some successes in creating microcapsules of peptide drugs that can make it past the digestive process in the stomach. They have also worked on delivery systems for injectable proteins, in an effort to extend the allowable period between drug injections.

Other approaches include protein administration via transdermal patches; in one fairly effective technique, proteins are coaxed across the skin barrier with an electric potential. Another idea is to chemically "toughen up" the protein molecule, using tricks from organic drug synthesis, so that the end product looks and acts like a protein molecule but is much more stable.

A more sophisticated method for delivering protein is probably not to deliver a protein at all, but to deliver instead a gene that codes for it. This drug delivery technique would involve using modified viruses to "infect" a patient with a manufacturing plant for the very medicine the patient requires. One problem, of course, is in switching the manufacturing process on and off. This can be done, but the technology is not ready for prime time.

There is nothing wrong with the concept of proteins as drugs. The big, frustrating obstacle is in positioning the protein drugs at sites where they can go to work to fight disease. Drugs that work well in a test tube or in tissue culture are often far less effective in the body. And to be approvable, obviously, a drug must be effective.

The short form is this: we are investing right now in an industry that has a diverse catalog of products but has not yet figured out how to deliver them. Pending solutions, and while we await the invention of a delivery truck, what are the investment alternatives? One approach is to look for biotechnology companies with products that are not proteins at all. Nucleic acids are candidates.

The nucleic acids RNA and DNA are formed from sequences of individual bases called nucleotides. In a strand of DNA, these bases are strung together like the beads of a necklace. The average human gene is a string of one thousand such beads. There are only four different types of beads in DNA, but the specific sequence in which they are strung constitutes the genetic code.

There is a Holy Grail in the nucleic acid drug business, a type of drug called a code blocker. The idea is to block the expression of specific genes that are blueprints for proteins that trigger or sustain various diseases. In principle, a code blocker would be a truly formidable weapon against cancer. This possibility has drawn a great deal of publicity and investor interest to this field. But this is science, not business. No one is manufacturing a code blocker today. Success, if it comes, is years away. Smaller, less ambitious new DNA drugs, however, can probably be brought to market in the near term.

Short, short sequences of DNA, created by stringing together two or three nucleotides, can have value as drugs. Even monomers have useful activity. These molecules are relatively small and tough. In the body they are somewhat at risk from enzymes that slice up DNA, but their survivability can be significantly better than that of a large, labile, and vulnerable protein drug.

Gilead Sciences, of Foster City, California, is using automated gene synthesizing machinery to randomly create trillions of different small DNA molecules — stringing together sequences of bases in much the same way as a lottery machine generates winning numbers. Each molecule produced by the machine is then tested to see which one binds most strongly to a protein molecule identified as a target. The object of the game is to find a drug that binds to the target molecule like Velcro. Binding will inactivate the molecule biologically and, it is hoped, inhibit or halt a disease process.

To develop and demonstrate this technology, a blood-clotting protein called thrombin was selected as a target. Gilead scientists used their mechanized drug production and screening technique to discover a unique nucleic acid molecule that binds to and inactivates thrombin. The Gilead molecule has some potential as an alternative to the familiar blood-thinning drug heparin. It may or may not succeed commercially, but it has pointed the way to a powerful method for creating drugs. Note that the company has not married its future to the development of some single blockbuster drug. It has a method, and a method is more important, strategically, than any one product.

One might call this the shotgun approach to drug development. It is done without much information about the shape or chemistry of the target molecule — by massively creating and massively trying out a trillion different potential drugs in order to identify one single drug with the strongest binding properties. Other strong players in the field of DNA drugs are Lynx Pharmaceutical, also of Foster City; and Isis and Genta, both of San Diego.

The opposite approach to Gilead's biochemical lottery machine is called rational drug design. To design a drug rationally, atom by atom, a chemist works from a clear picture of a target molecule and synthesizes a drug that he or she thinks will bind to it. It is like fine cabinetwork, like handcrafting a molding to fit a door, and much of it is cut and try and cut again and try again.

The leading company in this field is Agouron Pharmaceuticals of La Jolla. The company is subject to occasional starbursts of publicity. Agouron captured a worldwide media spotlight, for example, when it announced that it had completely determined the structure of an enzyme required for the replication of the common cold virus. The stock of course ran up, and subsequently ran back down when it became clearer to laymen that the company had not, after all, cured the common cold. Not yet. But they may indeed.

The first part of the problem is to achieve a clear picture of the target molecule. At this work the company excels. Agouron employs twenty X-ray crystallographers, probably the largest and most experienced group of such specialists concentrated at a single site. What a crystallographer does is determine the structure of a molecule. X-ray

crystallography is an old technology, but it has been powerfully aug-
mented and supplemented in recent years. It is easier to get a substantial quantity of purified proteins to work with, thanks to cloning.
When quantities in the range of ten to hundreds of milligrams have
been produced, the proteins can often be crystallized — the essential
gateway step to crystallography. Analysis of X-ray diffraction measurements from crystals has been made easier by faster and more powerful computers, and by the development of 3-D computer imaging and
other computerized modeling tools. As a sort of celebration of this
new technology, the company has even conceived a virtual reality
"molecular theater" in which scientists can be seated "inside" accurate molecular models.

Once a reasonable picture of a target protein has been drawn,
Agouron's chemists proceed to synthesize candidate drugs they hope
will bind to the target molecule and inactivate it. When the drug binds
to the target, however, the shape of the target may change significantly — and this of course changes the problem. When a carpenter
first try-fits a door, the doorframe remains true. Not so with fitting a
drug. Agouron is able, however, to create a new picture, this time of
the protein in combination with the drug, in order to see in atomic detail just how the drug is bound to its target.

This information enables the company to rapidly make and test-fit
a succession of new drugs, until the best fit is obtained. At no point is
the company deeply committed to any one molecule. It can cut its
losses, back up, try yet another new drug — or even abandon the target and try another concept. One analyst who follows Agouron stock
has made this the basis of his recommendation for it: "This company
is not going to be torpedoed by one product failure or by a failure to
receive an approval. They just keep on coming." Here again is the
value of developing a method rather than a product — a method supported by a technology that has been refined over time by an experienced team of cooperating specialists.

So far, none of the company's products has reached the market. In
trials are two experimental drugs in a class of anticancer agents called
thymidylate synthase (TS) inhibitors. The enzyme, TS, helps catalyze
the synthesis of thymidine, one of the four nucleotides necessary for
cells to synthesize DNA. Rapidly proliferating cancer cells require
high levels of TS, so by inhibiting this enzyme, it is hoped the drugs
can halt or slow the proliferation of cancerous cells. The drugs were

conceived (in a wise business decision) as an improvement on an accepted standard drug of this type, 5-fluorouricil, which has U.S. sales of about $400 million annually.

Among other drugs in prospect is an inhibitor for a viral enzyme that is involved in the replication of the common cold virus. This enzyme is an interesting target because it could possibly be effective against all of the one hundred–odd viral strains of the cold virus. Because of the way the enzyme works, it would be difficult for the virus to evolve "around" the drug to develop resistance to it. Of course, the drug does not yet exist. Agouron has passed along to Lilly a picture of the enzyme, albeit in somewhat reduced resolution. The company has structured its projects in such a way that the cost of basic drug research is funded by corporate partners such as Schering-Plough and Japan Tobacco. If this stock takes a dive on disappointing product news (and that cold virus story, precisely because it looks so promising, must also be understood as a setup for potential disappointment), you can confidently buy into the weakness.

Notice that the two higher-risk technology stocks noted here are producers of small molecules. Agouron, for example, makes molecules that are about one one-hundredth the size of a typical recombinant protein product, and one one-thousandth the size of an antibody. Small is beautiful at the moment, and I think this is going to be a helpful biotech investing principle until some of the protein drug delivery problems are solved. Side benefits of small molecules include strong patent protection and cheaper production. But the main present benefit is, smaller drugs can make their way to the site of a disease in sufficient concentration to make a difference. This helps their chances for early approval and commercialization. The larger the molecule — the more beads in the necklace — the greater the number of points at which the necklace can be popped.

The ultimate "method" biotech company is probably Human Genome Sciences (HGS). It is one of twelve (so far) new biotech companies hoping to profit by sequencing some or all of the human genome. This is obviously a venture investment fad. However, HGS seems to be running away with the business, for they are sequencing human genes at an astonishing rate. At the time of their public offering in December 1993 (they drew $25 million), the company reported it had already completed at least partial sequences for twenty-five thousand of the perhaps one hundred thousand genes that are to be found on the human chromosomes. The company is moving very fast because it has automated the sequencing process, using a battery of thirty-five DNA sequencing machines — but also because it is sequencing *genes* only. The researchers ignore so-called junk DNA, long stretches of genetic material that spans the distance between or interrupts the sequence of genes but does not code for proteins. HGS has an agreement with Smith Kline Beecham requiring HGS to give them a right of first refusal on all these genes, and for this privilege Smith Kline will pay, on a milestone basis, up to $50 million. They also paid an up-front fee of $13 million, and then bought a bit over a million shares of the stock offering at $31.60 per share. So HGS is a company that has made money from the start. If Smith Kline declines to develop a particular gene, Human Genome Sciences is then free to develop a product from it, or to seek another partner for further work on that gene, or to simply license it. But for a product Smith Kline does elect to develop and market, they will pay back to HGS a royalty of 6 percent.

It is impossible to quarrel with this arrangement. There are questions over what will become of the asset, the sequence library, in the patent process. But significant advantages invariably accrue to whoever arrives first for a gold rush, and I think these two companies were wise to seize the moment.

Technically, it's not quite right, in my opinion, to downplay or wholly ignore the junk DNA. This is the part of the human genetic sequence Human Genome deliberately skips in sequencing only genes. Junk DNA that interrupts genes, called intronic DNA, probably has some purpose, and many have been advanced by theorists. Since the intronic junk sequences are clipped out and left behind when a gene is translated, the cell is in effect taking notes on its translation activity. If you pieced together the snippets left behind by a dressmaker, you could assemble an outline showing what the dress looked like. In other words, in junk DNA one can discern the ratchets and spools of a machine capable of writing memory. This or some other junk-based mechanism may be of some practical use to the cell. So maybe all that junk DNA isn't junk and ought not be disregarded. This technical quibble does not diminish the economic value of the sequenced genes, of course.

One difficulty in buying shares of Human Genome Sciences is that the basic revenue stream, in the early going, is largely predictable and is therefore likely to be fully and fairly reflected in the market price of the stock. However, the company is opening box after box of Cracker Jacks, and it seems likely they will collect plenty of prizes from this work. Human Genome Sciences is a method company, and it makes money, and it will continue to make money without additional products or services until it runs out of genes to sequence. By then, it will probably have substantial streams of product and royalty revenues.

Chapter 19

Technology Tangibles

W E HAD IT from Marshall McCluhan that the art of every age makes a judgment of that age — as measured by the standards of the preceding age. For example, Picasso expressed his contempt for the great new age of technology by illuminating the devastated scene of his painting, Guernica, with a crudely drawn electric light bulb, its helical filament positioned in the frame, pointedly, where the sun should have been. He was expressing a judgment of his present based on the standards of his past — where else would such standards be sought?

We are now emerging from the age of mechanical technology — it is our own past, and its artifacts, which are mechanisms, are rather curiously becoming art. Some mechanical things are indeed quite beautiful and artistically made. They aren't making them that way any more, and with rarity comes appreciation in value.

Tangibles collectors have accepted and bought into the concept of mechanisms as art. There is a brisk market for fine mechanical watches. Carefully machined mechanical and optical instruments, such as gimballed navigation chronometers, surveyors' theodolites, and early laboratory spectrographs, are all strong collectibles. Old brass microscopes do well. The beautifully machined gyroscopic mechanical "brain" of a 1912 Whitehead submarine torpedo was recently auctioned at Sotheby's. Ferraris of a certain vintage have already boomed in price — and plummeted. In short, you can see how things are going. There is an emerging market in mechanical devices as objets.

Toy trains have long since gone through the roof. Lionel is good, American Flyer is better. For an ordinary Hudson locomotive train set that may have circled a Chrismas tree in the 1950s, we are now talking thousands of dollars.

There is a minor sociological insight to be drawn from the field of miniature steam trains — scale models, not toys — and it is this: the best of them have come from Japan. In the 1960s and 1970s, superb scale models of early American steam locomotives, produced in HO scale, were carefully manufactured of brass in Japan and widely sold in the United States. The center of manufacturing has now shifted to China and Korea, but the point is, you can pick up one of these little locomotives and marvel at length over its accuracy, workmanship, and intricate detailing. They are still doing fine mechanical work in the Far East. They seem in fact to have a great gift for it. Yankee ingenuity, it has been widely remarked, has gone east.

This is not a situation to be deplored. Mechanical technology (and manufacturing itself, including electronic manufacturing, is a mechanical technology) is indeed a thing of the past. It is not something we have lost and should endeavor to recover. It is a thing that is over, as a primary economic driver, and that is why it is being discussed here in the chapter on technological art and collectibles. It has long seemed to me that the idea that American business should emulate the Japanese, or "catch up" with them, is fundamentally wrong, retrograde, an appeal to American industry to go home once again. Well, you can't.

We are past the time to invest on the stock market in any hard device or technology that involves moving parts bigger than, say, a photon. Computer disk drives, for example, fall under this caveat. Investors are still imbued with the nineteenth-century idea that machines make products and products make money. The ultimate mechanical technology, for investors, seemed to be an idealized machine that would, once sold, consume more machines; the prototype was of course the safety razor and its consumable blades. A special class of machines that consumed machines were war machines.

Today's technology business, however, is increasingly based on creating and delivering images rather than products. It is the delivery systems — the networks — that are today's razors. Images are the blades. Manufactured hardware (including electronic hardware) is so easy to make it can rarely be protected. A manufactured product can be transformed into a commodity almost as soon as it succeeds, and at that point its success begins to fade into unprofitability. It is only as art that mechanical devices are good investments.

For interesting mechanical tangibles keep an eye on Sotheby's, which has full-time people in both horology and scientific instruments. In Princeton, New Jersey, at 129 Nassau Street, try Nassau Antiques. The owner is a skilled buyer of both European and American scientific and navigational instruments from the nineteenth and early twentieth centuries.

If you like classic cars, you may find them more affordable in miniature. L'art et L'automobile, a gallery of automotive miniatures, is housed in the New York penthouse of a retired racing driver, Jacques Vaucher. European, Japanese, and American "name" modelers of cars, engines, and chassis include Buzz Lockwood (engines), Gerald Wingrove (the Picasso of this business), Henri Biagent, Michele Conti, Marc Antonietti, and Fumio Sakai. Their little machines range in price from $1,000 to $25,000. You can also see at Vaucher's gallery some of the heroes of the great age of mechanical technology. A bust of Juan Fangio, seven-time world champion of the Grand Prix circuit, might interest you.

For steam-driven machinery, visit the Midwest. Once each summer near Traverse City, Michigan, steam tractor and stationary engine enthusiasts gather from all over the country. A 1905 Allis-Chalmers is a steam behemoth, maybe a little excessive for anyone's garage, but there are also fine large-scale models of steam traction engines. This seems to particularly intrigue English replicators of fine machinery.

For World War I airplanes, there are two major centers: Old Rhinebeck Aerodrome in Old Rhinebeck, New York, and the Lake Guntersville Aero Replica Fighter Museum, in northern Alabama near Huntsville. If you don't want a full-scale vintage airplane, check into the enormous collection of early aeronautica of Raceway Engineering in Riverhead, Long Island. Here you can pick up, for example, the finely built altimeter for a World War I Zeppelin. It reads to eight kilometers.

One of the most intriguing things about this field is that it is now possible to recreate, at a smaller scale, machines that have been lost.

Ron Phillips, who completed a career as a patent attorney for General Motors, has turned this into an enterprise. He obtained the original blueprints for early Ferrari, Maserati, and Mercedes racing cars. He puts the prints face down on a giant computer scanner, and the computer translates them into program instructions for computer-driven machine tools. The outcome? A 1957 Ferrari Testa Rosa, complete in every detail, including an ignition key that works and an operating V-12 engine — all reproduced at one-quarter of their original size.

How to maintain the collector value of such a readily reproducible work of art? Ron makes a run of twenty-five cars and then destroys the tooling. The tooling, in this case, is a floppy disk. He destroys it by simply erasing it. Ron's magnum opus to date was a Mercedes V-12 racer with an operating supercharger — he sold this car to Mercedes. These replicas have more than 1,500 precisely machined parts and sell for $40,000-ish. They are occasionally resold via Christie's.

Ron's work is an object lesson in the collectible value now arising from the mechanical technology of the past — and it is also a lesson in why this technology has become passé as a commercial enterprise. Mechanical work is too easy, and too easily automated, to occupy the hands and minds of millions, as it once did. For here is Ron Phillips, who is one talented guy but who is still, at the end of the head count, *one guy* — cranking out Mercedes Benzes in his basement. Any investors who are still in thrall to the concept of large manufacturers' advantages of scale and capital might want to give a little thought to Ron's considerable accomplishment.

PART THREE

TOOLS FOR INVESTING

Chapter 20

Sharp Players, Dull Winners

W HAT ARE WE REALLY trying to do here? Outsmart the market? Not exactly. What we are trying to do is *slightly* outsmart the market. To fully understand what this means, it helps to consider, as a working model, a different game.

There is a helpful lesson to be taken from the business of advertising packaged goods such as toothpaste, laundry soap, and cereal. You have probably noticed that television advertising for such products is almost unbearably stupid. Yet the advertising people who produce it are extremely bright. If you happen to meet one at a cocktail party, you will find him or her uncommonly witty, vivacious, intelligent. Why, then, is their flagship product, the TV commercial, so consistently idiotic?

Here's why.

Before they attempt to create a commercial to sell soap, advertising professionals first make a thorough survey of the kinds of people who happen to buy soap. From statistics they assemble a composite picture of the median soap buyer. This wholly synthesized person, the median purchaser, has two cars, 1.7 children, went to college for about 2.3 years, and lives in a middle-class suburb at the midpoint of Middle America.

Compared to the median purchaser and reader of books, that is, someone who happens to fall beneath the same bell curve as yourself, the median purchaser of soaps is a numbskull. This is why you in particular are appalled by TV commercials pitched at the tastes and interests of the median soap buyer. If the advertising people pitched their commercial to pique the (refined, intelligent) tastes and interests of you and me, they would sell a lot less soap. In their business, there is such a thing as being too stylish, too smart — and advertising professionals recognize it as a clear hazard.

How is the stock market different from the soap market? There is no difference. The stock market is also a mass market and it moves, by definition, in synchrony with the decisions of its median stock purchaser. When he buys it goes up. When he sells it goes down. We know he is in fact a he — but no one has ever seen this guy: the median stock buyer is a purely statistical construct. But it is obvious that this median person is neither the smartest nor the dumbest player in the stock market game.

And does he win, this mythic median player? He does not beat the market. If he invests he makes what the market makes, i.e., 10 percent. If he trades, he probably buys a popular stock halfway up the hill and sells it halfway down. This nets zero. The best traders do not try to emulate him. They try to get in and out two or three days before he does. But to anticipate him, you have to either be a lot like him, or study him as a specimen.

If the winning traders are close to, but not at, the median, it follows that players at the margins will lose. It is no surprise that an extremely dumb player will consistently lose. He buys too late and sells too late. But it also follows (rather less obviously) that the smartest player will consistently lose. He buys too soon and sells too soon. The too-smart player understands, long before everyone else does, what is going to happen to a particular stock. He acts on this information, and buys downtrending stocks while they are still in free-fall. This is called "getting in early." He sells too soon because he can clearly see the top coming long before everyone else does. This sensible selling forecloses on the gains to be made as the mass market mindlessly stampedes up the hill. As in the advertising game, there is a heavy penalty for being too damned clever. In advertising there is even a term for it: "too creative."

To win in the stock market, one must learn to anticipate, but only just slightly, the next play of the median player. This is the goal, the target, the objective: slightly better than ordinary thinking about the stock market. (One might call this preterordinary thinking — and it is a great gift.) There is no such thing as smart money. If you try to wholly outwit the stock market you have already, as a going-in position, outwitted yourself.

If you are not an innately ordinary thinker, then consider using some of the tools already honed by the advertising and marketing people: statistics.

The market itself is a statistical data gathering machine — constantly sampling and testing the opinions of stock purchasers about the values of stocks. Unlike the advertising people, you don't have to get on the phone to a picked population sample and conduct a survey — the survey is conducted daily between 9:30 and 4:00, and the results are reported instantaneously.

This notion of the stock market as a daily opinion poll has produced some folk wisdom that actually works. Tired homilies like "don't bet against the tape" are true and useful. If you cannot quite anticipate the median player's next move, just watch what he does and quickly do it too. Traders who buy stocks that are rising on heavy volume are basically riding the wave of middlebrow market opinion. The crest of the wave is the cap of the bell curve — the statistical median.

If you want to lead rather than follow the herd, the means are obvious. Books, computer programs, fundamental and technical reporting services, counselors — all these things exist to help you beat the market, supposedly through superior wisdom. The trick is, you must not become too wise. In both the ad business and the stock market, beginners do great. But beyond the beginning, the harder you try the more likely it is that your performance will deteriorate. It deteriorates with superior knowledge. If you become truly sophisticated about the stock market, you will so far exceed the skill level of the median player — that plodding, ordinary soul whose moves are identical with those of the market itself — that you will lose almost all the time. This squares with conventional wisdom. Dullards and geniuses alike turn out frayed coats.

But it is frustrating. It defies our mothers' teachings that hard work and application are rewarded, and that slackers are not. If you work too hard at the market you will quickly work yourself right out of the winner's circle. The market does not reward hard work. It rewards the ability to anticipate, ever so slightly, median thinking.

There are two morals. First, if you start to lose, walk away from the table. Forget stocks for a while. Come back fresh. Try to recapture some of your original naiveté — your beginner's luck — by ignoring the market.

Second, if you cannot walk away, focus constantly and heavily on statistical measures of the market — with a clear understanding of what you can hope to learn from them. Like the advertising professionals, you must use statistical information to try to plot the position of the median players in a mass market. These median players are neither smart nor dumb. They are somewhere midway between these two extremes — and so is the stock market.

Chapter 21

The Top Funds, the Best Options

T HE OBJECT OF THE GAME is to discover a strategy that is ever so slightly smarter than that of the median investor. Knowing this, the next step is to evaluate the relative merits of the investment vehicles available to us: stocks, funds, and options. This chapter will treat funds and options. For a start, on the next page is a list of the top ten mutual funds in science and technology over the span of a recent twelve-month period. In this particular period, the average return of the top ten technology funds was 21.23 percent — and it is quite typical, that is, not an exceptionally good or bad result for a technology portfolio.

Which one should you buy?

But wait a minute. Why buy any of them? There is an argument to be made for picking stocks instead of funds. The argument is simply that funds buy too many stocks; you need not.

Small mutual funds can do quite well, but they attract new money in proportion as they succeed in the market. For a "hot" fund the new money must be allocated, and it isn't long (instants) before the fund manager buys many more than sixteen stocks.

More than sixteen is too many. In a large cap mutual fund, the number of stocks in the fund's portfolio may rise into the hun-

THE TOP TEN TECHNOLOGY FUNDS

12 months' relative performance ranked by 1-year gain

	Assets Under Mgt (Mils)	One- Year Gain	Five- Year Gain
Fidelity Select Computer	61.5	40.75	188.19
Fidelity Select Electronics	45.6	39.86	204.18
Seligman Communications	93.0	39.72	178.30
Merrill Technology A	134.3	35.68	0.00
Merrill Technology B	141.1	34.23	0.00
Fidelity Select Technology	229.8	29.34	190.68
John Hancock Freedom Global Tech A	41.7	27.06	77.91
T. Rowe Price Science & Technology	500.3	23.52	203.54
Alliance Technology	174.7	23.30	142.59
Invesco Strategic: Technology	251.6	17.85	189.62

dreds. There is no advantage to the customer in such superfluous diversification. It does not reduce risk. It does reduce return by averaging down the impact of the best few stocks. Thus, for mutual funds, as for certain kinds of stocks, success itself can be self-liquidating.

Picking stocks is about as much trouble as picking funds. (It is widely observed that there are more mutual funds to choose from than there are individual stocks listed on the New York Stock Exchange.) Go to the library and pull down the current *Value Line* report on stocks. Open it anywhere. Then pull down Morningstar's report on funds. Open it anywhere.

The pages are graphically almost identical — densely packed with difficult information. Is stock selection more complicated than fund selection? It doesn't look like it, and it isn't. Evaluating a portfolio containing multiple stocks (that is, a fund) is by definition much harder than evaluating any single stock. The moral: if you are going to take the trouble to pick something, pick stocks instead of funds. The risk is the same and the potential return is better.

The great marketing strength of funds — which is supposedly diversification for small investors — is actually a major weakness of the larger funds. Do not passively accept the idea that a professional manager will do better than you at picking stocks. Some of them may indeed have superior knowledge of their craft. But as noted in chapter 20, superior knowledge and diligent work may actually damage the manager's performance. And in a large fund, he or she will be applying stock-picking skills every day to the massive purchase of stocks neither of you needs to own.

Thus, if you prefer fund selection to stock selection, try to pick a small one. If it succeeds too well and grows portly, as they are wont to do, extract your money and shift it back to a younger small fund, perhaps with a value of $20 million or less.

Yet this is not quite the whole story. The largest funds also work, sometimes even better than the smallest. This is perhaps because of their brute force buying power.

In a period of very low interest rates in 1993, the fund industry began to draw money at rates exceeding a billion dollars per day. During this same period of fund-buying mania, the rate of open-end stock fund formation reached four new funds per day. Notwithstanding the financial services industry's eagerness to cash in on the funds' magnetism for money, by inventing new funds, most of the incoming cash favored a relatively few well-established, historically top-performing funds.

Gigantic funds have the power to bootstrap, and this is one reasonable explanation for their appeal and success. What is bootstrapping? It works like this. Say a relatively small growth fund has a very good year. It will quickly achieve stardom by popping to the top of the rankings published by fund-rating services. Fund buyers buy performance, and most of them buy it rather blindly, so a top percentage gainer will attract a great deal of new money.

What happens to the new money? The fund manager will probably deploy it very quickly to purchase more shares in the most favored of the stocks he or she already owns. Up they go. As the stocks go up, the fund's performance gets better. More good publicity follows. More money comes in. More incoming money is plugged into the purchase of the fund's favorite stocks. And the cycle repeats. Nothing succeeds like success.

There are various ways for this magic circle to unwind. It does not work indefinitely. In a bear market, the cycle goes into reverse as artificially inflated stocks collapse, fund investors redeem their money, and the fund manager must sell to meet the redemption demands. The bubble poppeth.

In a persistent bull market, the fund can simply wind up owning too many shares of too many stocks, in which case its performance will begin to mirror that of the S&P indexes, and it will no longer draw in fresh money with exceptional percentage gains. A fund cannot beat the market after it *becomes* the market.

Nevertheless, because of their buying power, large funds can overpower for a time the problems inherent in the fund concept. So add the large funds to the list of investment possibilities, so that it includes both the very small and the very large. With this in mind, let's take a second look at the top funds, this time sorted in order of their asset holdings:

THE TOP TEN TECHNOLOGY FUNDS
ranked by assets

	Assets Under Mgt (Mils)	One-Year Gain	Five-Year Gain
T. Rowe Price Science & Technology	500.3	23.52	203.54
Invesco Strategic: Technology	251.6	17.85	189.62
Fidelity Select Technology	229.8	29.34	190.68
Alliance Technology	174.7	23.30	142.59
Merrill Technology B	141.1	34.23	0.00
Merrill Technology A	134.3	35.68	0.00
Seligman Communications	93.0	39.72	178.30
Fidelity Select Computer	61.5	40.75	188.19
Fidelity Select Electronics	45.6	39.86	204.18
John Hancock Freedom Global Tech A	41.7	27.06	77.91

Notice that the five-year performance numbers draw the line of a suspended hammock, that is, performance sags toward the middle of the list. The long-term top fund performance numbers are clustered at the top and the bottom of this list.

If we ignore the midsized funds in favor of the largest and smallest, two funds with interesting records pop out: Invesco Strategic from near the top of the asset list, with $251 million under management; and Fidelity Select Electronics from near the bottom of the asset list, with $45 million under management. Both funds have excellent long-term performance records, as indicated by their five-year gains. T. Rowe Price is also interesting, but I have a deep-set aversion to buying from the top of any list. Any number-one performer is pressured to regress toward the mean. This is a statistical principle that is usually illustrated with sports analogies. Ask yourself, for example, what the chances are that the winner of this year's Rose Bowl will repeat the performance next year. Any first-place performance is exceptional. Exceptions are uncommon, and exceptional events are not usually repeatable.

As an additional criterion in fund selection, consider technological diversification. Technology-sector funds typically own too many stocks of just one kind. If you are attracted to the idea of investing in a science-and-technology fund, it would make sense to look for one that has invested in a range of technologies, including both hard (semiconductors, electronics, computers) and soft (biochemicals, software). The difficulty is, most technology-sector funds, including some of those noted in the tables presented earlier, still define technology in the terms of the 1960s and 1970s: they tend to be heavy in electronic technologies, light in biology-based technologies. To diversify adequately, you should perhaps pick two funds, one calling itself a science-and-technology fund, and the other a health-and-biotech fund.

You might also wish to consider mixing a selection of technology stocks (your own selection) with a good biotech fund. I suggest Fidelity's biotech sector fund. Here, the idea is to use the purchase of a biotech sector fund as a substitute for the purchase of your stock allocation for this group — the idea being to split the risk across a basket of stocks. But in my opinion it would be better to buy your own biotech basket, following precepts suggested in chapters 17 and 18. The five core stocks are obvious, and you need only three to five higher-risk issues to fill the basket. If you buy the sector fund, you will in this way purchase too many biotech stocks.

What about options as an investment vehicle?

If you can be consistently right about the twists and turns in a particular stock, you can turn $100 into $1.5 million in as few as six successive option trades. The vehicle is easily available: options on technology stocks can be picked up for $75 to $250 the contract. In this game you can put $1 in and take $5 out. If you can do this time and again, reinvesting each gain, then here is the progression in value in your account:

$100 initial stake
500 after 1 trade
2,500 after 2 trades
12,500 after 3 trades
62,500 after 4 trades
312,500 after 5 trades
1,562,500 after 6 trades

No one I know has ever actually done this — the odds against it are formidable. On the other hand, why rule it out as a possibility? It is an easily demonstrated fact that in an option contract you can easily double your money in a few hours — or lose it entirely. And per the superb advertising slogan for the New York lottery, "Hey. You never know."

In science-and-technology stocks, the use of option contracts became widespread in the early 1980s, coinciding with an enormous speculative surge in technology stocks that ended with a bang in 1984. Options can be used conservatively — that is, as an inexpensive device to conserve capital in a sharply downtrending market. I began using put options for the first time in 1984. A put contract goes up in value as the underlying stock goes down. It is, in effect, a side bet on a stock's demise. That year I bought puts as the technology market nosed into decline, and as we were stopped out of long positions in one technology stock after another. Our option positions did not represent a heavy capital commitment, but they kept us afloat in a hurricane market.

The experience gave me a new and more positive outlook on the option trading scene. It may indeed be a casino in the view of most investors, but in the science-and-technology sector I think the option market is a tool you can and should investigate. At their most volatile, technology stocks can be a real handful. Options can make a portfolio of such stocks a little more manageable. When the market is clearly trending up, stocks make sense. But when it starts jerking and lurching downward, you can use options to protect yourself.

Whether the potential reward is sufficient to offset the risk is something each investor must decide — but not in the abstract and not casually or from prejudice. The way to decide is with the help of a computer program designed to evaluate, in the real world, the risk, volatility, and value of the many option contracts available to you in the technology field. For a start, try OptionVue Systems of Vernon Hills, Illinois, for a tutorial diskette called Options Made Easy. Then decide.

Here is some detail on how to use options in a down market. When a technology stock takes a dive, it usually happens so fast that you can take no meaningful action — on that day. Say you own a software stock trading around $39, and it suddenly drops to $32. Do nothing. Allow several days for the stock to stabilize. At some point, short sellers — who will be buying the stock to take their profits — will have bid it back up to around $35. On that day sell your stock and buy some put contracts at the $35 strike. Technology stocks typically retreat in two successive plunges.

Amgen, Biogen

The second plunge may take this stock down at least $5 and possibly $7. But this time you're short, meaning you'll make money on the second sudden decline. Sell the puts at $30 or $28. In this way you can recover the money you lost on the initial sharp failure of the stock, plus a little. And you're out of the stock. Instead of "waiting it out" for months for the stock to recover, you can put the money to work in more productive positions. The net effect is the same as if you had sold at the exact top.

Options on science-and-technology stocks are traded on the Chicago Board of Options Exchange, the American Exchange, the Philadelphia Exchange, and the Pacific Stock Exchange. The household words of high technology — Microsoft, Lotus, Apple, Amgen, Biogen, and so forth — are all optionable, and so are many of the less obvious stocks in this sector. Scan the Pacific Exchange list for less commonplace stocks. Because it is a San Francisco exchange, it is a little better attuned to the science-and-technology stock and option markets than the others.

Chapter 22

Pencils Are Over: How to Pick Stocks

THERE ARE TWO WAYS to pick stocks. The first is to look around you, read widely, listen, pay attention, and hope to capture a stock "idea." Maybe a broker calls with this idea. Maybe you hear it at a cocktail party. Maybe you happen to notice it in a magazine or trade publication or professional journal.

This method may work or it may not, but the approach is haphazard, with an emphasis on the hazard. As you can well imagine, any stock your friends and neighbors are likely to talk about (brag about, to be candid) over lunch or at a cocktail party is a stock that has already gone up.

The stocks they do not talk about are the ones that went down. Your broker probably won't talk much about the losers either, so verbally received stock information is not much help. The accepted idea is to buy low and sell high. You need to know about the stocks that are down — not the ones that are up. They got there, down, by sinking. How do you discover downtrodden stock bargains if the only stocks people ever talk about are the ones that have already made them lots of money?

Information from published financial information resources, like lists of hot stocks published in the daily newspaper, follow this same wholly irrational pattern. A senior commodity trader once told me that "if you're reading about it, it's over, forget it." His advice rings true for stocks as well.

The other (and much better) method for picking stocks is massive elimination. Start out with the universe of all stocks (about ten thousand are actively traded) and systematically discard every single stock you don't want to own. The few stocks that survive this process of systematic elimination are the ones you might consider "discoveries." This is the method I suggest you use: massive hurling away. With a computer it will take you just a few minutes to do the whole job.

Serious investors tend to be of a certain age and demographic profile, with the result that many of us are either uneasy with computers or have had to learn to overcome that uneasiness. The first generation that is truly comfortable with these machines is just reaching majority. There are now almost 200 million computers in the United States; the computer population is catching up with the human population. Yet one group most likely to benefit financially from computers — the investors — still strongly resists or dodges using them.

Until fairly recently, there were very good reasons to resist. Investment software, much of it too complicated to use, proliferated in the mid-1980s as hobbyists and traders jumped into the game of computerized investing. At one time there were more than 350 programs made available to investors, mostly for charting and technical analysis of stocks. At this writing, the field has sharply contracted. Only a few good programs survived the shakeout, and you need to buy only one or two. I suggest you start with Telescan, a reasonably priced computerized investment database from Houston. You also need a modem.

Computers do two things for investors.

First, a computer turns numbers into pictures. Instead of scanning a printed table of the earnings of a company over the past five years, you can graph these same numbers and see, instantly, whether they trend up or down, and whether the stock price faithfully follows. This visual process is much more pleasant than doing arithmetic.

Second, the computer can "do sorts." For example, it can rank all semiconductor stocks in order of their sales growth. It can rank biotech stocks in order of stock price gains. It can rank software companies in order of earnings achieved — and projected earnings as estimated by professional financial analysts.

One program such as Telescan, and the database that supports it, should give you most of the tools you need to successfully pick science-and-technology stocks. It puts on your computer screen stock quotes, a twelve-year price history, earnings histories and estimates, reports of trading by company insiders, news wires, and much more. It is not comprehensive or highly sophisticated. It is completely adequate for most individual investors, and it makes the problem of computerizing very simple: (1) Buy a computer. (2) Subscribe to Telescan and read their straightforward manual.

And then what?

For our purposes, the first thing you should do with the program is use it to eliminate all stocks that are not science-and-technology stocks. Use Table A as a checklist for the program. Mark the industry categories you wish to include, as in the table. In picking these industry groups you are automatically excluding all the low-tech and non-tech stocks. With this first simple step, you have already eliminated from consideration several thousand stocks. (If you find this a bit draconian or too narrow in scope, note that the program is a general purpose database, and you can use it anytime as a tool to explore investments in every category.)

The computer is now able to dial up Telescan's database and scan through it, looking only at the qualities of science-and-technology companies. (It will not dial Houston, but will connect via a local number in your town.)

Table B is a list of scanning criteria that you can use to pluck from the database a short list of stocks that may be attractive buys. The database will return to your computer a list of stocks that meet every one of the criteria listed. The criteria are demanding, and so the list will be short.

The instructions seem cryptic or programmatic, but just key them into the system letter by letter. Here are the principles involved.

The first criterion is *no debt*. We meet it by scanning for companies with a debt-to-equity ratio of zero. Long-term debt is poisonous for technology companies. They should be able to fund their growth by selling products or stock. If they have to borrow a great deal of money, it is quite possible that something has gone wrong.

The second criterion is *market capitalization*. I suggest a lower limit of $25 million. If you go much lower, you are going to start picking up companies that are too small and speculative. Technology investing is high-risk investing, but this does not mean we are shopping for risk. To the contrary, we are eager to limit it as much as possible.

TABLE A. TELESCAN INDUSTRY CATEGORIES
IN SCIENCE AND TECHNOLOGY

Industry	Group
Aerospace	Defense Equipment
Aerospace	Defense
Computer	Local Area Networks
Computer	Memory Devices
Computer	Services
Computer	Graphics
Computer	Mainframes
Computer	Mini/Micro
Computer	Optical Recognition
Computer	Peripheral Equipment
Computer	Software
Computer	Integrated Systems
Electronics	Measuring Instruments
Electronics	Semiconductors
Electronics	Control Instrumentation
Energy	Alternate Sources
Engineering	R&D Services
Instruments	Scientific
Lasers	Systems/Components
Machine Tools and Related Technologies	
Medical	Drugs
Medical Drug	Diversified
Medical	Instruments
Medical	Biotechnology/Genetics
Medical	Generic Drugs
Office Equipment and Automation	
Pollution Control	Equipment and Systems
Protection	Safety Equipment and Systems
Telecommunications	Equipment
Telecommunications	Services
Telecommunications	Cellular
Utility	Telephone

Require that earnings per share are greater than zero. Simply put, this stipulates that all companies identified by the computer must be profitable.

Require a P/E ratio greater than 10 and smaller than 30. This criterion will exclude stocks that are priced far from the median.

Now use the computer's power to put things in a certain order. Not only can Telescan return a list of stocks that meet your criteria — it can rank them. The last item noted in table B, sales growth, will rank the companies per this criterion.

TABLE B. SCANNING CRITERIA
1. Debt/equity ratio = 0
2. Market capitalization > $25 million
3. Earnings per share is positive (no losses)
4. Price/earnings ratio is between 10 and 30
5. Sales growth over 5 years ranks highest among all those companies meeting the four preceding criteria.

Now submit the list and wait a few seconds. Telescan will return to you a selection of stocks like that in table C. You can easily save it in a file on your disk and print it out on paper.

This list will be short, and you should accord it some importance. A "short list" of profitable, fast-growing, debt-free companies has a lot more intrinsic value than a piece of plain paper.

Work with the top of the list, say the top twenty-five. These will be the fastest-growing companies in terms of revenues, although not necessarily in terms of earnings. We are requiring positive earnings, but we are not emphasizing earnings growth in this simple scan. (If you wish to do so, however, the program is rich with criteria you can use to identify and characterize earnings growth.)

On another piece of paper, sketch one of the simple statistical bell curves of P/E ratios as described in chapter 4. (Okay. So pencils are not *entirely* over.) This will give you a reasonably accurate sense of prevailing technology stock prices on the particular day you are doing this work. Pull a vertical line through the cap of the bell-shaped curve.

TABLE C. TOP 5-YEAR SALES GROWTH PERFORMERS				
Company Name	Market Cap (Mil)	Earnings per Share	Price/ Earnings Ratio	5-Year % Sales Growth
Zilog	$620	1.6	21	138
Lattice Semiconductor	340	1.2	15	59
Electronic Arts	880	0.9	18	44
DIGI International	210	1.0	14	36
Amtech	150	0.9	11	35
Intervoice	260	0.6	23	31
Tseng Labs	130	0.4	15	24
New Image Industries	60	0.5	22	22
Legent	840	1.4	16	19
Acuson	420	0.5	26	12

Note the corresponding P/E ratio. Let's say it's 20. Now define a range of plus and minus 5 points. This means you should pay closest attention to the stocks on your list with P/E ratios ranging from 15 to 25. This is the "blind spot" of the market. It is where you are probably most likely to discover a bargain.

Among the companies with the fastest-growing revenues, you may discover five to ten stocks that meet this pricing criterion.

Telescan can chart stocks on your screen. Use this capability to take a look at each of the stocks on your short list. See table D. Price charting is a practice strongly associated with stock trading, but this program charts, in addition to price and volume, a number of criteria of interest to investors who want to know the fundamentals. In the chart shown, notice the stair-step pattern bracketing the stock price history. These brackets are calculated and displayed in order to show you the historical limits placed on a stock by its current earnings.

TABLE D. P/E RATIO AND OVERLAY

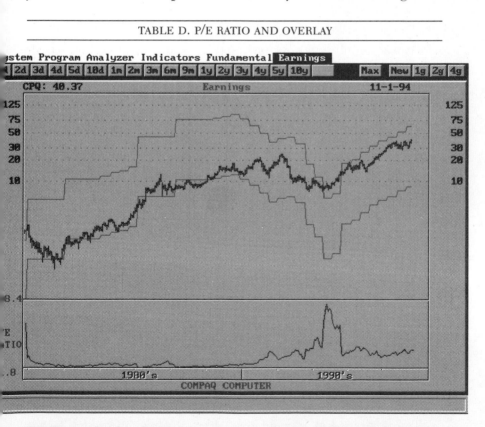

P/E ratio may be plotted in Analyzer as a graph and an overlay. The overlay creates an undervaluation/overvaluation channel, which shows the fluctuations of the ratio over time. Below is a maximum span stock graph with the P/E ratio and overlay.

The brackets answer this question: what would this stock cost today, given the current earnings, if it were trading today at the highest P/E ratio it has ever attained? Conversely, what would it cost today if suddenly, in the next ten minutes, it sold down to the most depressed P/E ratio ever attained?

These reference lines are helpful in guessing how far an uptrending stock might climb, or how much of a loss you might see in case of a reversal. It thus shows you upside potential, downside risk — and how far the stock has already come. Finally, it shows you where you might have to sell. It is a good practice to have some sort of selling price in mind on the day you buy a stock. The program is not restricted to drawing P/E brackets. It can create similar lines using other price-per ratios, including price per sales and price per cash flow. If you pay attention to such lines, you will sharply reduce the odds of buying at the exact top, and increase your chances of buying somewhere near a low.

The chart will also show you what traders are doing with the stock. You can accomplish this by drawing various traders' lines. Learn to do this from the program manual. It is simple, and it will enable you to sample a large body of market opinion about your stock of interest. (A Fibonacci fan might sound like a fashion accessory item, a little something to accent a ball gown, perhaps — but it is in fact a button you can push to learn what the traders are about to do to your stock.)

Associated with the stock chart are panels of fundamental data, including balance sheets and accounting ratios. Check to be sure that the company has adequate coverage of assets over liabilities, two to one or better. Look for lots and lots of cash. This is the most important asset in technology.

Telescan's news wire contains recent press releases for all the major companies in its database; the releases usually conclude with the phone number of the investor relations or financial officer of the company. Once you have narrowed the list to just five or ten stocks, read their news. Call them up and request information on the companies, their technologies, and their histories. If you ask, they will often throw in recent reports from various brokerage analysts. You may wish to visit a company as well. An especially promising sign you have done the job right is that the company will be slightly amazed to hear from you.

The point is, do the qualitative, subjective part of the job *last* — after you have used the computer to eliminate all the stocks that are obviously unworthy of consideration. Let the computer show you which few science-and-technology stocks are actually attractive as buys.

Meantime, if your broker should call to urge upon you the latest hot "hi-tech" stock (another Amgen, another Microsoft, another Intel) you can tell him you have already run a comprehensive computer scan and his hot stock didn't surface, for some darn reason. If it did indeed surface, of course, consider it. But not many do. There are ten thousand stocks out there. You want to own only sixteen.

Telescan is attractive because it is a one-stop shop for the many different types of information you need as an investor. It is also extremely flexible. You can use many more sophisticated and varied scanning criteria than those suggested in the simple protocol presented here. You can, for example, scan for stocks that have been asleep for a long time but are suddenly skyrocketing. You can call up a list of stocks that move opposite the S&P 500. It is a complex and highly adaptable program.

As a technology investor you may wish, however, to develop some additional or alternative capabilities — specifically, a private database. This is easier than you probably think it is. To construct a financial database on your computer, you will need one of the standard packaged PC database programs such as dBASE or Paradox. There are a couple of good reasons to go to the trouble it takes to create a private or "guerrilla database" of this type.

First is cost.

Six weeks after the close of each major reporting quarter — on January 15, April 15, July 15, and October 15 — quarterly earnings reports flood into the pages of *The Wall Street Journal, Investor's Daily,* and *The New York Times.* The value of these data, were you to download them with your computer, would add up to about $300 per day, and the reports keep coming in a torrent, day after day, for a couple of weeks. Each day, as you release your newspaper above the garbage can, you might count off to yourself: $300 . . . $600 . . . $900.

To recapture some of this value, you can load the earnings digests into your computer. For each company, you need only basic items of data: the revenues, the net income, and the earnings per share. The published digests report these values for both the current quarter and the year-ago quarter, so there are just six numbers to enter for each company of interest. With good dexterity and a well-designed interface, you can load earnings reports for six companies per minute into your computer. At the Princeton Portfolios, we load about 350 reports during the flood-tide period of earnings reporting.

This is not, of course, purely an exercise in saving money. It is an exercise in making money. The value of these data, sponged right out of the newspaper, decays rapidly as commercial databases make the same information available on-line to other analysts. But, surprisingly, there is an advantage of as much as six weeks to be gained here. During this period, you can make comparative evaluations of technology stocks with some confidence that the information you produce has not already been completely discounted into the markets. You can augment this data with balance sheet information (like debt, cash, assets and liabilities) gleaned from widely available printed sources such as the *Standard & Poor's Stock Guide* or *Value Line*.

What should you do with such a database?

The best way to initially rank technology stocks is by sales growth. This is the first signal of success. You can obtain sales growth numbers from Telescan, much as in the sorting protocol outlined above, but it is a derivative number drawn from twenty successive quarters of historical performance. To detect recent and early performers, a calculated value based on the most recent versus the year-ago quarter's revenues will prove helpful. Your database can be programmed to calculate the percentage revenue gain and to record this result even as you enter the raw numbers.

As a first step in processing your data, find the median P/E value for the whole, 350-plus stock database. The database can be programmed to draw the bell-shaped curve for you, so you don't have to sketch it. Note by "good eye" the P/E ratio corresponding to the peak. Interesting companies will have prices within plus or minus five points of the median value.

Have the computer identify for you and list the top one hundred stocks per *recent* sales or revenue growth — and set all the rest aside. Other sorting criteria are itemized here. The approach is slightly different from that used with the Telescan program, but the objective is the same. The idea is to winnow from the initial large list of several hundred stocks those few — perhaps fifteen — that are actually potential buys.

- Determine earnings for the top one hundred. Then jettison all the companies with losses.
- Construct a ratio of earnings growth to sales growth. Eliminate companies with extremely high and extremely low ratios. For example, if a company's sales growth is double its earnings growth,

then it is in a high-volume, low-profit business (like a discount computer store). This is not a desirable thing. Similarly, a company that produces good earnings from flat sales may be well managed — but it is not a runaway success. Not a keeper.

- Construct a ratio of long-term debt to sales. Rank all one hundred companies in order of this ratio, and throw out the nine most heavily indebted companies per this criterion. By using a ratio, you are including a few companies that would be eliminated by a less lenient, no-debt whatsoever criterion.
- Construct a ratio of sales to shares. Rank the stocks and throw away the companies at the lower extreme of the ranking. They have put too much stock on the market. Supply will swamp demand, and the stock will move like a slug.
- Create a value index. We use a simple point system that rewards strong revenue growth, good current earnings, good earnings growth, a small amount of stock on the market, and a low price as measured by various price-per ratios. When you rank the remaining stocks on your list by a value index, you pump the bargains to the top of the list.

From this point, the investigation is essentially the same as that outlined for the Telescan database above. The product is a short list of stocks that you must carry into the "real world" by examining each company's news, management, technology, analysts' opinions, and business relationships.

It is interesting to play around with databases using different criteria. Two slightly different protocols are presented above, using two different databases, but you will find that in any given quarter, you can use multiple protocols of radically different design — and nevertheless keep coming up with the same short list of neat stocks. In other words, attractively priced, high-quality companies will rise to the top of the pot, and this will happen just about any way you choose to stir the stew.

This is reassuring in a way, but it also shows you how important it is to work fast. Every serious-minded market professional uses computers to winnow lists of candidate buys. As you scrutinize the companies whose names appear at the top of your short list, you can be pretty sure that someone else is simultaneously scanning the top names on a very similar list.

This is why we try to capture data early — so that the population of onlookers will not yet be too large. If you work at it, you can still hope to get a little ahead of the game, which is the optimum thing to do. In a major reporting period you have at most a six-week lead time in which to load your data, working maniacally, before everyone else in the world starts freely downloading the same information — downloading it at the speed of light.

Chapter 23

When to Sell

O N TELEVISION, guests of financially oriented programs are frequently asked the question, when do you sell? The question sounds utterly basic, and a quick, crisp answer is always forthcoming — usually a neat little dogma such as "we sell on earnings declines," or "we sell on a 15 percent stopout." The very succinctness of both the question and the answer supports the widespread idea that for this question of when to sell, there indeed exists an exactly right answer. There is none. No one knows when to sell.

Most people never sell, and their portfolios do well over time because the centerline trend of the market is up. Prices swing around the centerline, but they average to a steady upward progression. Three steps forward, two steps back. Net gain: one step. Since the late 1920s, the market has returned on average 10 percent per year. Since World War II, the return has been somewhat higher.

The idealized practice of selling out at tops and buying back in at bottoms is called "timing the market." It is supposed to be a method of making a fortune. Perhaps it would work if you could time the market perfectly, but no one can. It is evidently possible to time it very well, but this has an unexpected result.

The practical payoff for timing the market very well (as opposed to timing it perfectly) is in safety, not profits. Mark Hulbert, a *Forbes* columnist who has analyzed the portfolio profits and risks of successful timers' portfolios, has suggested from his historical data that the main benefit of expert timing is simply that it reduces volatility. The portfolio swings are damped. The extra gains actually achieved, after commissions, are not impressive. So before considering the question of when to sell, you might better ask whether to sell at all.

For technology stocks, the answer is yes — do sell — but only occasionally. You should sell when you are pretty sure that a monopoly has been breached, or when a once novel product has been transformed into a commodity. Don't lose sleep over the problem of technical obsolescence. Technology products usually become commodities long before they become obsolete, so I would suggest you lose sleep over that instead.

Obviously you should sell any stock when its price exceeds its true value. The trouble is, technology stocks are growth stocks. This makes it difficult to fathom what their true value might be. Value cannot be measured, in the traditional manner, as a function of the company's stream of earnings — very often technology companies have no earnings. Any loose money is instantly plowed back into the company to propel further growth.

Selling such a company on news of an earnings decline, as from two cents to one cent, is a trivial exercise. It is also unhelpful to sell technology stocks on a goal system, i.e., sell on any 100 percent gain. It is not unusual to see a fivefold appreciation in a technology stock, and not impossible to see a tenfold gain. That's why people buy them. But there is no easy way to set "realistic" goals for such stocks.

For these reasons technology stocks tend to be sold on technical signals. Put another way, you should sell if the stock's price declines too much. But how much is too much? Understand clearly what we are talking about here. There are no techniques with the power to predict the future course of the stock market or of any stock. You can predict only that which you can control. You can perfectly predict your intentions. What you can do with a computer is determine in advance what a reasonable selling point would be. Where should you draw the line?

A rational answer to this important question can be discovered with the help of a computer program called an optimizer. An optimizer can determine which trading rule has the best record, over a period of many years, for calling the tops and bottoms on a particular stock or index.

Optimizing programs first surfaced for microcomputers in 1983, but the recent availability of truly powerful microcomputers has brought the technology along very rapidly in the 1990s. The number of such programs in use by investors is now in the thousands, enough to suggest the programs themselves have become a force in the market.

Using an optimizer is a good example of using statistical information to plot the course of the market. The program will not attempt to make a value judgment about what the smart thing to do might be — nor will it attempt to rule out the dumb thing to do, for the market very often *does* the dumb thing. Instead the program will simply tell you how the market has acted historically, statistically, given today's circumstances.

Suppose you own Intel, and you would like to follow a simple retracement rule: sell on, say, a 15 percent pullback. You may instruct your broker to sell your stock at a particular price calculated in this way. Placing such a stop-loss order is a common practice. But would a stop-loss set 16 percent down work better than one set 15 percent down? (The answer is yes, incidentally). Or should the figure for percentage retracement be dialed up and down with some other market factor, such as volatility?

Optimizers do the sheer, brute force computing involved in answering such questions. Running an optimizer is not very exciting. Your computer may simply sit and think for a day before it prints out, in a single short burst, the best strategy.

Optimizing programs are available from Pardo Corporation, in Northbrook, Illinois; and RTR Software, in Research Park, North Carolina. The Telescan service discussed in chapter 22 also offers an optimizer.

If this is too sophisticated for your taste, then just sell by the seat of your pants. A helpful guide is that traders' rules of thumb, like the famous 15 percent retracement, are usually almost, but not quite, right. The reason is logical. What happens at –15 percent is that all the people following the –15 percent rule sell out. This often exhausts the selling pressure on the stock, so that it never reaches –16 percent, but instead majestically turns around and starts going back up.

If you simply add a percentage point to the familiar traders' rules, you can usually create a better rule. When the whole technology group is in decline along with the market, as for example in response to an international crisis, a 27 percent retreat is expectable and allowable. The Dow, in a correction of this type, might draw back only 16 percent. So if you are setting stops, you will need to be more generous in allowing for swings in the typically volatile science-and-technology groups.

If you are transfixed by the idea of buying and selling — trading as opposed to investing — there is some more advanced help available in the form of technical trading software, including some experimental platforms you can use in devising your own rules for selling.

Three programs I like are Patterns, from NAVA Development Corporation in Lewiston, New York; Stock Prophet, from Future Wave Software in Redondo Beach, California; and DesignCad 3-D, from American Business Software in Oklahoma City, Oklahoma. All are intended for IBM-compatible machines.

Patterns is a pattern-recognition program used primarily by day traders. But in some sense we are all day traders on the particular day we elect to buy or sell a stock — hence the appeal of this powerful and well-conceived program. It makes a microscopic examination of daily price patterns for whatever predictive value they may hold.

The idea underlying the program is familiar. For example, most experienced investors have noticed that a long downtrend punctuated by a tremendous one-day downspike in price usually marks a bottom. Similarly, an upspike in price after a long steady uptrend often marks a top. This topping pattern is so widely recognized that it has a common name: it is called a blowoff top.

Most one- or two-day price patterns are far less obvious, but many of them have strong predictive value as markers of sharp turns in the market. It is also true that the most commonly recognized patterns are often meaningless — or meaningful for one stock but not for another. Run the Patterns program to learn which trading patterns are actually worth watching for.

On any given day, a trader using Patterns can ask the program to determine whether the preceding few days' trading has ever, in the past, anticipated a big upturn or downturn. The program methodically chugs through the entire price history of the stock, and produces a report that (1) identifies the pattern as one that has historically been important or — in many cases — unimportant, and (2) displays the odds favoring or opposing today's proposed stock purchase or sale.

I have noticed lately the statistically inspired idiom of the Patterns program creeping into the conversational style of traders. Increasingly you hear phrases like ". . . I went long with 73 percent confidence in the pattern," and you can guess from this that they are checking the Patterns program. If you have already decided for fundamental, technical, or strategic reasons to buy or sell a stock but are waiting for the right day to come along, Patterns can pinpoint that day for you. An excellent demo disk is available.

Stock Prophet is sort of a shamanistic program. Its role is to make the ways of neural networks comprehensible to mankind. Neural nets are increasingly used to formulate buy/sell strategies. Nets are in use at institutions such as the World Bank, Nikko Securities, and Fidelity Management. They are practical tools, and they work. What they do is examine the relationship between the price of a stock and a select handful of other indicators. The price of a gold mining stock, for example, is clearly influenced in varying degrees by many other things: the price of gold is an obvious factor, but so too are the prices of oil and of currencies, and the tenor of the bond markets. Similarly, utility stocks are always affected by the cost of money and the cost of energy — semiconductor stocks respond to the book-to-bill ratio. But precisely how?

A neural net program generates, from multiple indicators, a single helpful indicator with predictive value for a stock or index. The indicator is simply a line on a graph that goes up and down, just like a priceline on a stock chart. But the indicator line will turn up or down perhaps ten days in advance of the turn of the stock. The neural net's guess may be right or wrong — obviously, it cannot peer into the future — but it will always make an intelligent guess, based on all the available numbers.

You could derive a similar and perhaps even better guess using conventional statistical methods — if you happen to relish statistics. Wasyl Malyj, who created a neural net that recognizes blood clots under a microscope, described in chapter 15, told me he regards a neural net as a sort of electronic statistician; not nearly as good as the real thing, but adequate for the given purpose. Most investors are interested in the result, not in statistical details, and for them the neural net is just now beginning to make sense. Neural nets used to require tricked-out computer systems and a total intellectual immersion in the technology. No more.

Today, thanks to the current generation of powerful computers, and also thanks to the Stock Prophet software from Future Wave, neural nets can be run from the top of your kitchen table. Stock Prophet is not a neural net. It is a translation and data packaging program. It enables investors to use the familiar language of investing and trading to set up, run, and read the results produced by a neural net program. The actual neural network software, for which Future Wave is also a dealer, is Brainmaker — a well-recognized neural net "engine" from California Scientific. California Scientific is located in Nevada City, California.

Never mind these fantastical names, incidentally. These are down-to-earth products. Future Wave's Stock Prophet isn't really an oracle, of course. But it is the next best thing — a well-informed guessing machine.

If you are conversant with computers, you may prefer to do the work of Stock Prophet yourself. A mutual fund timer in Oregon uses the RTR Technifilter as a "front end" for her Brainmaker, and reports excellent success. Technifilter is substantially less expensive, so if you can deal with the steeper learning curve, it is the more economical and capable choice.

DesignCad 3-D is a reasonably priced 3-D program intended for engineers and architects, but market experimenters are increasingly using it to devise three-dimensional graphics. This idea is, as always, to figure out where you are. Two dimensions are adequate to graph price versus time, as in a simple stock chart. But for problems involving three variables, you need three dimensions. A 3-D chart can be useful if you are invested in a derivative such as a simple stock option. Here the relationship between the price of the option, the price of the underlying stock, and the time remaining until the option's expiration can be painted on the screen. DesignCad 3-D responds to programming language already familiar to many investors and computerists, the BASIC language. If you can use BASIC, you can make DesignCAD 3-D draw a graph of your particular problem.

Charting packages that graph in 3-D for financial applications are called, generically, FiCAD software, and they are becoming increasingly popular among market traders. Banks are offered such packages on a lease basis for up to $950,000 per year. The street price for DesignCad 3-D is about $300, flat. It has a nice backup capability, which is that if you should ultimately despair of using it to trade the financial or derivatives markets, you can use it to design a new garage or arrange your furniture.

Chapter 24

What to Expect of the Twenty-first Century

HE STOCK MARKET is a school that teaches us to watch for pendulum swings — not absolute changes. The idea that we have now entered a postindustrial age sounds intriguing, but surely it does not mean the absolute end of industry. So what *does* it mean? More specifically, what does it mean to the purchaser of stocks?

What it seems to mean is a swing in the society: away from the mass production of identical, stamped-out products — toward the diverse production of a great new variety of different products. We are emerging from a long, deeply peculiar era in which commercial standardization, which was necessary for human progress, set artificial limits on human variety. The variety of commerce is now finally catching up with the diversity of people.

Computers have made it easier and quicker to redesign and retool for short manufacturing runs. Companies are no longer required to commit (or overcommit) great sums of borrowed capital to the development of single lines. Products can have shorter lives and still make money. Some can utterly change in function — without retooling or any physical alteration whatsoever — the computers and other devices that can be defined and redefined by their software. The concepts and rituals of new product introductions, cycles, and obsolescence are going away.

Product monomania — Henry Ford's obsession with reproducing his Model T forever after — is ebbing out of the system. Absent the dictates and rigors of mass production, manufacturers now have a certain amount of creative freedom, and they are beginning to play with it. It is significant that an attorney in Detroit is successfully manufacturing several different types of historically important motorcars — in his basement. One can read this as a signal that manufacturing no longer means mere replication on heroic scale, and has a much lower threshold of entry, from a capital standpoint, than it once did.

Individualized, "targeted" marketing to diverse groups of customers is replacing the stamped-out mass marketing pitch of the mid-twentieth century. The emergence of cable television, and the contraction of broadcast networks, is probably a reasonable prototype for the twenty-first-century economy. Broadcast television tried to sell everyone in America a Chevrolet and a can of cold beer. But on cable, a variety of different products can be sold to a variety of different people with a variety of different interests.

As manufacturing production becomes more various, the producing companies will trend to a smaller size. It is easier to go into business now. The term *advantage of scale* will be redefined, for the real advantage of scale now appears to lie with nimble companies of relatively small scale, i.e., in the 100-to-400-employee range. In due course the idea of a giant corporation will begin to seem strange. Companies of skilled people may form ad hoc, via computer networks, exist for a time to solve specific problems — then dissolve. You can see this as the Balkanization of big business, or as a positive step back toward human individuality. Either way you choose to interpret it, it is happening. Insofar as possible I avoid investing in companies with a market capitalization greater than $1 billion. In technology, big is not beautiful. Big is hulking.

Purely technological trends are also in progress. Transportation is being supplanted by communication. (Why send a salesman to Cleveland at 650 miles per hour when you can send his image at the speed of light for a lot less money?) Commerce in things that are heavy (bridges and buttresses, steel and coal and oil) is giving way to commerce in things that are light — electrons and photons.

Not only will mass production give way to diverse production — mass services will give way to custom services. Medicines will ultimately be manufactured in the clinic using machines to create molecules appropriate to the unique chemistries of individual patients. There will be fewer and fewer blockbuster drugs, blockbuster movies, blockbuster food fads. There will be more specialized products marketed to groups of individuals who share special needs and interests.

From an investor's standpoint, the promise of specific products is already less important, today, than the promise of methods for creating products. Companies that make products that make it easy to create other products are good investments. Xilinx and Lattice, who are making it easy to create new semiconductor circuits, are good examples. Gilead Sciences, which has created a technology that creates DNA drugs — by the trillions, actually — is a better bet than any company locked into the development of any single would-be blockbuster drug. Parametric Technology, one of several companies that automate the processes of mechanical design, by enabling the engineers to visualize mechanical devices on a computer screen, is another good shot.

Some of the great networks, which traditionally have been the wellsprings for wealth based on technology (broadcasting networks, airline networks, telephone networks), will evolve by interconnection into supernets, and will thereby lose their power to monopolize. However, the creation of protected access *within* public networks, by means of encryption technology, will produce prodigiously successful new businesses, including important new monopolies.

Computerized education is becoming a business because it fills a need. This need is for useful information — information that makes money and rescues lives that would be wasted without it. The media and services of computer-borne education will be increasingly good businesses to invest in. All sorts of concentrations are diffusing. Concentrations of knowledge, in universities and great libraries, can now freely diffuse into the society by electronic means. Workers concentrated in factories and offices are diffusing into their own homes.

Stock traders and investors can anticipate great numbers, blockbuster numbers, but they will arise from the creation of variety, rather than the massive replication of sameness. There will be even more IPOs, less funding and refunding of bonds, less long-term capital investment absolutely, and more fluid, short-term activity in the stock markets. Money will accomplish more but move faster. The physical stock exchanges will close forever, supplanted by computerized trading media. Investors will become more like traders — the pendulum swings now in the direction of higher account turnover: more frequent buying and selling in order to keep pace with an economy in which variety and rapid change are the only fixed features.

What to expect of your own portfolio? A realistic target is an averaged performance of 19 percent per year, and particularly astute or fortunate investors may see up to 25 percent per year extending over two- or three-year stretches. And in any given single year, it is quite possible to achieve a 100 percent gain, usually on the strength of selecting that year's one or two "hot" science-and-technology stocks.

Index

P.H G.   – QUALCOMM
          – G. M.